ADVANCE PRAISE FOR
Autobiography in Shakespeare's Plays

"From November 1604 until Shrove Tuesday 1605 the Master of the Revels chose to stage seven of Shakespeare's plays, all dealing with justice and law, equity and mercy, courts and jurisdiction: *Othello, Merry Wives of Windsor, Measure for Measure, Comedy of Errors, Loves Labours Lost, Henry V,* and *Merchant of Venice*. W. Nicholas Knight argues this was no coincidence: Tilney used the plays to teach the proper use of law to the new King James. In this pioneering study of Shakespeare's life and work, Knight discovers new sources for the plays—the lawsuits and family concerns of Shakespeare himself, matters which may well have inspired Shakespeare then and heighten certain fresh thematics now. This is a unique work of legal history and theater criticism showing how each may illuminate the other."

Arthur F. Kinney, Director, Massachusetts Center for Renaissance Studies,
University of Massachusetts, Amherst

"W. Nicholas Knight has made exciting discoveries where law and literature intersect in Shakespeare's plays. This book persuades me that the 'allegory' Shakespeare made of his life carries important and dynamic traces of the troubles, legal and familial, that beset the playwright's daily thoughts in the 1590s and beyond. This is a pioneering work of scholarship and detection in the field!"

Tony Connor, Department of English,
Wesleyan University, Connecticut

Autobiography
in Shakespeare's Plays

For Carolyn
and her devotion to literature.
Best Wishes
Nick (and Diane)
Knight
8/24/02
Rolla, Mo.

Studies in Shakespeare

Robert F. Willson, Jr.
General Editor

Vol. 6

PETER LANG
New York • Washington, D.C./Baltimore • Bern
Frankfurt am Main • Berlin • Brussels • Vienna • Oxford

W. Nicholas Knight

Autobiography in Shakespeare's Plays

"Lands so by his father lost"

PETER LANG
New York • Washington, D.C./Baltimore • Bern
Frankfurt am Main • Berlin • Brussels • Vienna • Oxford

Library of Congress Cataloging-in-Publication Data

Knight, W. Nicholas.
Autobiography in Shakespeare's plays:
"lands so by his father lost" / W. Nicholas Knight.
p. cm. — (Studies in Shakespeare; vol. 6)
Includes bibliographical references (p.) and index.
1. Shakespeare, William, 1564–1616. 2. Dramatists, English—Early modern,
1500–1700—Family relationships. 3. Dramatists, English—Early modern, 1500–1700—
Biography. 4. Shakespeare, William, 1564–1616—Family. 5. Fathers and sons in
literature. 6. Shakespeare, John, d. 1601. 7. Autobiography in literature. 8. Land
tenure in literature. 9. Self in literature. I. Title. II. Series.
PR2893 .K58   822.3'3—dc21   2001042485
ISBN 0-8204-3777-8
ISSN 1067-0823

Die Deutsche·Bibliothek-CIP-Einheitsaufnahme

Knight, W. Nicholas:
Autobiography in Shakespeare's plays:
"lands so by his father lost" / W. Nicholas Knight.
–New York; Washington, D.C./Baltimore; Bern;
Frankfurt am Main; Berlin; Brussels; Vienna; Oxford: Lang.
(Studies in Shakespeare; Vol. 6)
ISBN 0-8204-3777-8

The paper in this book meets the guidelines for permanence and durability
of the Committee on Production Guidelines for Book Longevity
of the Council of Library Resources.

Printed in the United States of America

For my wife
Diane Lowline Knight
and her creative inspiration

OLIVIA.   A comfortable doctrine, and much may be said of it.
          Where lies your text?

VIOLA.   In Orsino's bosom.

OLIVIA.   In his bosom? In what chapter of his bosom?

VIOLA.   To answer by the method, in the first of his heart.

OLIVIA.   O, I have read it; it is heresy. Have you no more to say?

VIOLA.   Good madam, let me see your face.

OLIVIA.   Have you any commission from your lord to negotiate
          with my face? You are now out of your text. But we will
          draw the curtain and show you the picture. Look, you, sir,
          such a one I was this present. Is't not well done?

VIOLA.   Excellently done, if God did all.

OLIVIA.   'Tis in grain, sir; 'twill endure wind and weather.

VIOLA.   'Tis beauty truly blent, whose red and white
          Nature's own sweet and cunning hand laid on.
          Lady, you are the cruell'st she alive
          If you will lead these graces to the grave
          And leave the world no copy.

OLIVIA.   O, sir, I will not be so hard-hearted. I will give out divers
          schedules of my beauty. It shall be inventoried, and every
          particle and utensil labelled to my will:

                              Twelfth Night. I.v. 217-241

Acknowledgments

I wish to thank Mary Reynolds for her preparation of the manuscript; Lori Gray, my student assistant; and Prof. Robert F. Willson, Jr., Editor of the Series for his reading of and suggested changes in the text.

Permission for quoted passages have been kindly extended by

David Bevington, editor of *The Complete Works of Shakespeare*, Addison-Wesley Educational Publishing, Inc., N.Y.

Eric Donald Hirsch, *The Aims of Interpretation*, University of Chicago Press, 1976

Northrup Frye, *Anatomy of Criticism*, 1973 and C. L. Barber, *Festive Comedy*, 1959, University of Princeton Press, Princeton, N.J.

David M. Bergeron, *Shakespeare's Romances and the Royal Family*, University of Kansas Press, Lawrence, Kansas, 1985

Bruce L. Lockwood aand *Yale Journal of Law and the Humanities*, "The Good, the Bad, and the Ironic: Two Views on Law and Literature", Vol. 8:2, pp. 533-58.

Table of Contents

Introduction

"I am myself the matter of my book," Montaigne wrote in 1580 in his
preface. He knew by then what he had not fully known when he started
to write his *Essays* eight years before: that any book is bound to be a
book about its author. This necessity became his conscious purpose. But
because his goal was not yet fully clear, he called his book *essais*, that is
to say *tests* or *trials*: trials, as he tells us later, of his judgment and his
natural faculties.

Before he finished, Montaigne's concept of his book had greatly
expanded. He said that you cannot write about yourself without writing
directly or indirectly about all mankind. His subject became a twofold
study of himself and of man, with the purpose of finding the way for
himself to live and principles of living for others.

Donald M. Frame[1]

Shakespeare read Montaigne's *Essays* in his colleague John Florio's
English translation (1603). In fact two copies of the *Essays*, one in the
Folger and one in the British Library, contain his signature, and the
Folger's also was signed by his great granddaughter.[2] At the time of
the English translation English authors were emerging from behind
their works as Jonson was creating his *Works* out of his dramas, and
Shakespeare's British Library copy contains marginalia noting "Here
the Author speaks of himself." Shakespeare's works, even his sonnets
in the first person, are not clearly autobiographical. Nevertheless,
Shakespeare's plays contain autobiographical material. Furthermore
these elements, more than the chronology of the plays, evidence not
only thematic concerns and preoccupations but elements of his life
present in his Life Records and are, hence, beyond doubt autobiographical references. These hereto ignored artifacts from Shakespeare's life
in the plays are the subject of this book.

In his study, essentially of Shakespeare's tragedies, C. L. Barber[3]
finds this method of explication "compelling," establishing parallels
in *Hamlet* with my earlier "exhaustive and moving account of John
Shakespeare's legal difficulties in decline," taking them (I.iv. 23-33)
to be a description of the dramatist's own father. The father-figure as a
key element in the evolution of Shakespeare's tragedies is a main
thesis of Barber's analysis. His earlier *Festive Comedy*[4] is a stimulus
for the following analysis of Shakespeare's self-referencing, mostly
found in his comedies, but not absent from the tragedies, the romances,
or the histories. The theme being focused upon here is inheritance. In
his early works it tends to be appropriately from the point of view of
the recipient, whom Shakespeare would have been (*Comedy of Errors*
to *As You Like It*); through the crisis created by losing his male heir
(*Twelfth Night* and *Hamlet*); to manipulating law as the preserver
and giver, as he finally became of his estates to his daughters (*Measure*

for Measure to Tempest). Thus, the theme of inheritance is present from beginning to end in his works.

What is of interest to the general reader of these periodic conjunctions between the plays and his life is that they now make impossible conjecture that someone other than Shakespeare wrote the plays. No one else lived William Shakespeare of Stratford's (1564-1616) life. No one else could have fabricated these references either by forging the records or knowing and copying them in his lifetime. Also these references cannot be referring to completely other events than what is available in the life-text. The data come from sources in Stratford, London and Westminster and are in church, court, personal, state, literary, as well as public documents. They are in addition birth, marriage, death, and publication records (Stationer's Register), court cases and juristic references in diaries, Inns of Court records, the Stratford Court of Record, Queen's Bench, Chancery and performances before legal audiences in Gray's Inn, Middle Temple Hall, Greenwich Palace, Banqueting Hall, and Hampton Court as well as the Globe.

We have to be cautious what we say about how Shakespeare felt, or what he was trying to do. However, the context provides the play with its place of performance, source of the text and its alterations if parallel to the tone or purpose found in facts of the life record. These can suggest obvious intent, or provide evidence of concerns, welling up into these textual artifacts. We even have audience response to corroborate some purposes. Names, addresses, similar events between his life and his plays repeated over time substantiate a pre-occupation. Here even common sense allows us to put two and two together. Whether we are reading or seeing the plays, discussing or producing them or teaching them, we cannot longer ignore the author who existed and infused his plays with his personal presence.

To ignore his presence is to, inexcusably, contribute to the false idea that we know little about him or believe that he had no clear personal or intellectual ideas of his own. The following insights may bring us closer to discovering why great minds during his life were, and since are, willing to give so much of their time to him; not merely to be entertained, but to learn some important things about humankind, and in a developmental sense through the entire course of his plays. We may discover why and when he wrote particular works in conjunction with his life concerns and how his attitudes changed or were modified. What got him going? What kept him going? Why did he stop? As my wife, Diane, so clearly made me see in our discussions about life with our four daughters, three sons, twins (as he had twins) and grand-daughters and grandsons, there are life patterns in his plays present in his own family which contributed to making him so teachable.

Often we are preoccupied only with Shakespeare's literariness. We obliterate the autobiographical facts instrumental in producing his versions of literary works in the first place. These frequently appear early in each play from legal or juristic evidence; hence the following book also enters the new, exciting, and controversial field of law and literature initiated by White, Weisberg, and myself at MLA in the early '70s[5] and recognized as, in Shakespeare studies, bearing fruit by Posner, Kornstein, Sams, and Rockwood in the '90s:[6]

> . . . law and literature is a catholic discipline, a "big tent" that encompasses tendencies, but is still undergoing some growing pains. To help law and literature find its voice, reach a wider public, and achieve its communitarian potential, law and literature scholars need to find a synthesis between [Daniel J.] Kornstein's [*Kill All the Lawyers: Shakespeare's Legal Appeal*. Princeton, 1994] text-driven enthusiasm and [Ian] Ward's [*Law and Literature: Possibilities and Perspectives*. Cambridge, 1995] theoretically meticulous approach. Law and literature scholars need to reach out beyond the boundaries of academia and inspire a new generation of readers in the virtues of our constant and constantly changing civic culture. In this way they can translate what is good and useful in their ideas and approaches into a language that can reach and move the widest possible audience. Law and literature must combine a commitment to teaching with a renaissance in the spirit of the public intellectual if it is to achieve its full potential.
>
> Bruce L. Rockwood[7]

The purpose of this study of autobiography in Shakespeare's plays, wherein land his father lost and Shakespeare compensated for, but not without other difficulties, is to find the connecting theme. Ultimately, Shakespeare had to seek mercy and equity before courts of law and justice. This conjunction of law and literature produced some of the best thoughts and sayings of mankind cited today even in American Supreme Court decisions. We can, it seems to me, appreciate Shakespeare as a source for discerning human patterns or recurring personal problems and their possible resolutions for humankind. At any rate, this is why I have devoted my life to teaching him to all ages. The following study, hopefully, will reveal that Shakespeare, as that source of enlightenment for us, was making discoveries in his life from his own fiction.

January 1, 2001
W. Nicholas Knight
Old Farm c.1859
Rolla, Missouri 65401

Chapter I

Shakespeare's Court Case[1]

... who, by a seal'd compact,
Well ratified by law and heraldry,
Did forfeit, with his life, all those his lands
Which he stood seiz'd of, to the conqueror:
Against the which, a moiety competent
Was gaged by our king; which had return'd
To the inheritance of Fortinbras,
Had he been vanquisher; as, by the same cov'nant,
And carriage of the article design'd,
His fell to Hamlet.
... to recover of us, by strong hand
And terms compulsatory, those foresaid lands
So by his father lost:

Hamlet. I.i. 86-95, 102-104

Mary Arden, Shakespeare's mother, brought to John, her husband, an estate from her parents that was to have become William's, but his father lost it. This would be of no literary interest and only passing biographical import if William Shakespeare had chosen not to refer to it in his dramatic works. Although little noted, there is no doubt that he does so explicitly from *The Taming of the Shrew* to *King Lear*. What is of critical, interpretive significance is how we can discern and what we can garner from the implications of his father having done so.

It is with considerable reluctance that a reader, let alone a critic, wishes to engage in the revealing of autobiographical data. For some reason, the desire is to keep Shakespeare's works immune from the author and the author immured from his own life. This has not occurred for Milton, Spenser, Marlowe, Sidney, or for authors of other periods. Relationships between Spenser and Ireland, Milton and his marriages and his Secretaryship, Marlowe and Kyd, Sidney and his family exist and are all discernable in their works. We have denied Shakespeare this richness of context.

This even goes to the extent of denying that William Shakespeare of Stratford and London wrote the plays or that there was an author (or that we can speak of the entity at all). There is evidence Shakespeare of Stratford existed from the Life Records, and the Last Will and Testament mentions his fellow players in London. Nevertheless scholars have to indicate they side with those who accept that there is an author, and that this person was William Shakespeare of Stratford and London, living from April 23, 1564 to the same day in 1616. Richard Dutton says of Shakespeare, he..."remains the dominant voice in the English-speaking world's construction of its definitive author--a voice essentially of preprint culture, of closet or privileged readership,...as well as the 'theatrical' Shakespeare".[2] The author producing the autobiographical references in Shakespeare's plays is not the construct of his actors, editors, fellow poets or critics, indicated by Barbara A. Mowat[3] but the person writing the text of the plays who refers to the passages in the Life Records, the figure Ben Jonson clearly indicates was his familiar contemporary playwright.[4] Alexander Leggett believes Shakespeare covers his tracks,[5] but the following study suggests he does not entirely. The difficulty of finding Shakespeare, let alone the author, in his works, as we shall see, is that he reveals his personal presence rarely and usually only at a moment of crisis in his life and in the play's plot. Furthermore we must be reminded that the nature of the public-personal author was only emerging or redefining itself at precisely this cultural moment, as attested to by the above critics.

As has been pointed out to me by Robert F. Willson (Professor of English at the University of Missouri-Kansas City and the gracious editor of this volume), E. D. Hirsch and the genetic critics[6] (*The Aims of Interpretation*, University of Chicago Press)--argue so well for 'inner' textual and 'outer' normative horizons of meaning that are created and controlled by the author (p. 2). Citing Lucien Goldman, Hirsch says the illumination of a meaningful structure constitutes a process of comprehending it, thus giving it *meaning*. While insertion of it into a vaster structure is to explain it, giving it *significance*. In other words, the meaning comes from the interpretation of the text. To relate the literary text to biographical data or legal documents is not to alter its meaning as explained but to make it significant by comprehending its relationship to personal history or legal proceedings from the author's life. These connections have been denied by literary theorists, particularly the New Critics, who deplored the use of biographical or historical information. Hirsch goes on to say:

> Therefore, let me state what I consider to be a fundamental ethical maxim of interpretation, a maxim that claims no privileged sanction from metaphysics or analysis, but only from general ethical tenets, generally shared. *Unless there is a powerful overriding value in disregarding an author's intention (i.e., original meaning), we who interpret as a vocation should not disregard it* (p. 90).

Court documents and life records should not be ignored when seeking the significance of literary text in addition to its meaning. Thus we have foregone the discovery and inquiry into the complicated process of conflicting intentionality from which Shakespeare's products came.

We move from *reading* to *interpretation* by questioning that very unity of subjectivity and intention that we have postulated in order to read. We do this by exploring the cultural codes invoked by the producer of a text and by looking for signs of counter-intentionality,[7] division of purpose, the return of the repressed, in the text before us....It would be an astounding thing if an extended body of written work did not reveal signs of divided consciousness — as if everyday life had no psychopathology, and civilization no discontents. In some other world, perhaps, but not in ours can such a state of affairs prevail.[8]

Spenser's care and hostility over Ireland in relationship to Book V of *The Fairie Queene* is present in his *View* and personal court cases. Milton and Mary Powell are obviously connected to the sonnets, Eve, and his Divorce Tracts. Philip Sidney, his sister and a female in exile from Elizabeth's court can be found in the two *Arcadias*. Much of Marlowe's text and the texture of his works come from the fabric of his own dramatic life. Wherein is the surprise, then, that Shakespeare's concerns about twins, inheritance, law cases, losses, daughters and other familial preoccupations are evidenced in his plays?

...Shakespeare's plays, for instance, seem to hang there complete by themselves. But when the web is pulled askew, hooked up at the edge, torn in the middle, one remembers that these webs are not spun in midair by incorporeal creatures, but are the work of suffering human beings and attached to grossly material things, like health and money and the houses we live in.[9]

Virginia Woolf gives us good precedent for our insights into Shakespeare's texts. As much as they must have been shaped for their cultural, social, dramatic, commercial, aesthetic and generic purposes, the "thingness" of their art[10] like a stone in a path is apparent when lines from a personal court case or an address of a relative appear in the dramatic text.

If it were only to point to Mary Arden's name, for example, appearing as the title of the wood in *As You Like It*, this book would not need to be written and I would not invite the reader into still further investigation. Only coincidentally does the data show that the author of the plays must be William of Stratford. Much more importantly, the sequence of these references parallels developments in Shakespeare's important case and striking happenings in his immediate family. Beyond this biographical data and authorial self-referencing in the plays is the area of exciting exploration where attitude, tone, tension, compensation, resolution and self-examination may be determined. The placement, extent, and recurrence of this autobiographical content can be seen to give impetus and frame to plot, viewpoint to narrative, tension to structure, and ultimately crisis to language.

By no means does the following investigation attempt to characterize or psychoanalyze the author or a play definitively or comprehensively. On the other hand, it will attempt to lay out a process for not only finding a coherent concern, autobiographically grounded, in any given play but also connection and progress, or at least movement, of these autobiographical preoccupations throughout the *oeuvre*, and across, predominantly, Shakespeare's comedies. Because the thread of connection relates to law, there will be several symbiotic outcomes wherein life-text through both dramatic and legal language experiences desire, manipulation, betrayal and reward. These two language systems evidence periods of anger and disruption, balance and compensation, self-analysis and objectivity. Read and interpreted together they provide Shakespeare's conjunctive experience through juristic and dramaturgical language, fictional compensation for real losses and linguistic power, in the face of life's ephemeral entities. He lost a son; he gained a monarch's attention. In turn his dramatic language could interpenetrate legal language.

Working with Shakespeare's life records, I began looking for personal and legal content that crosses over into the text of the plays. His concern for twins and the loss of his twin son appears in *Comedy of Errors* and *Twelfth Night*. Some of the legal transactions involved in loans, purchases, and wills in Shakespeare's life appear in the text of *Merchant of Venice*. However, on further investigation, the play seems to reach for the deeper concerns surrounding these personal matters, such as losing a mortgage on a bond, failing to secure a purchase, a loss of a child, and securing deeds of gift to insure inheritance. The text seems to be working not just with vocabulary in certain legal categories known to relate to Shakespeare's dealings but to include feelings and emotional involvement of specifically similar content between the text of the play and Shakespeare's personal losses and possible fears around the composition date of 1596-1597. Given this possibility, then, perhaps some of the tone, characterizations, and themes, particularly the court actions toward Shylock, might receive some clarifying explanation from the experiences Shakespeare was enduring while writing this controversial play. Does it help our understanding of the play if Shakespeare lost the child who was to inherit his estate; had his income threatened; lost his inheritance in a court case on failing to pay a bond; could have lost his house at this time; and saw his father threatening the lives of people he owed money to, and may have needed to be converted from his recusancy as a Catholic in order to leave his house and join the Church of England society of his town? We have, possibly, up until now looked too far afield into sources, historic events, and social attitudes of his time to fully explain the personal energy that transformed the varied sources of the plots into Shakespeare's powerfully conceived link between intolerance and the capitalistic fear of loss. Thus, as we acknowledge in most writers, but not of Shakespeare, there are examples of the dramatist's text being influenced by his life experiences.

Nothing proves the liveliness of Shakespearean scholarship better than its controversy. Therefore I would like to take this opportunity to make some respectful comments on unfortunate implications in Virgil K. Whitaker's important paper on "Shakespeare's Use of Learning: Where are We?", presented at the Shakespeare Association of America's meetings in Pasadena in 1974. Dr. Whitaker's essential point is "...that research, whatever its area, should seek to explain the play."[11] Difficulties surround the definition of "the play" and where, how, when, and under what circumstances it exists. These aside, Whitaker's implications were good-humoredly supported by Robert B. Heilman's Second Annual Shakespeare Lecture, "Shakespeareanism: Similitudes and Inquiries", criticizing innovative approaches to Shakespeare at the same meetings. Both speakers appear at heart to be advocating a kind of professional monism to facilitate the judgment of criticism upon its goals and methods without considering its differing fruits. It is obvious that the Universal Genius, his plays' infinite variety, and his negative capability have and will continue to tease sound scholars into different directions; albeit sometimes out of thought. I let other Shakespearean researchers obligated to source and comparative studies; historic, political and theological backgrounds, linguistic, numerological and poetic patterns; and archetypal, anthropological, and psychological interpretations of the author or the plays defend their interests in their respective methods. For, there is no reason why the mainstream of Shakespearean criticism cannot pursue, forever, an explanation of the play without insisting that "whatever its area" all Shakespearean research must do so. Such an assumption places many approaches, goals, and findings in unwarrentedly pejorative states of being. Other types of research may, as by-products, yet provide new and worthwhile contributions to our growing knowledge of how or why the plays were written.

Such a field in question would be that of Shakespearean biography and of this study, surprisingly, autobiography. Few, if any, of our undergraduate or graduate students demonstrate any knowledge in this subject and many continue to believe, therefore, that little is known of

Shakespeare's life. The result is to leave this tradition of Shakespearean scholarship out of their teaching at all levels, lending credence to rampant Baconism and Oxfordianism on the part of the public. Do our students know that Shakespeare had twins, or a son named Hamlet? How many of us still insist that his son's name was "Hamnet"? (His namesake, Sadler, spelled it with an "l" on official documents, as on the second page of Shakespeare's will.) We sometimes suggest that the students read a Shakespearean biography, but how often are they asked to do a paper on the problems arising from having done so? I suspect there may even be Shakespearean scholars who have never read a biography of the dramatist; or, for the most part, only ones written before this century, or by authors regarded as nonacademics (Marchette Chute and Anthony Burgess). Leslie Hotson's and, particularly, A. L. Rowse's work have received considerable scorn from these quarters, or indifference. We have many biographies but none is regarded as definitive, authoritative, or even a classic; these are rather viewed as popular or even novelistic literature. The professional exceptions are two scholarly compilations (but nonbiographies), those of Halliwell-Phillips (*Outline*) and the basic (but in need of updating and correcting) two-volume work by E. K. Chambers. We look to these and to S. Schoenbaum's work for their reproduction of primary source materials, not for any finished narrative. Such a project should be as much a concern for Shakespearean scholars as a definitive edition of any one of the plays.

Recent work and discoveries by Samuel Schoenbaum and Mark Eccles indicate that this area of Shakespearean research is being opened up again to our benefit. Schoenbaum's monumental *Shakespeare's Lives; Shakespeare: A Documentary Life*; and *Shakespeare: Records and Images* divide fact from fiction, and establish some truths and deny such myths as the deer-poaching episode that supposedly forced Shakespeare to leave Stratford. These painstaking works are necessary preliminaries to the production of a new life of the dramatist employing all our modern techniques, methodologies, and analytic skills. Mark Eccles' investigations into Shakespeare's friends in Warwickshire, particularly Thomas Greene, Shakespeare's lawyer-cousin who lived with the Shakespeares in New Place, and Philip J. Finkelpearl's *Marston of Middle Temple*, about the theater at the Inns of Court and Greene's connection with Middle Temple and the Marstons, are proof enough how much can still be recreated of Shakespeare's contacts, sources, and immediate social milieu and how these influenced his intellect, his concerns, as well as his plays.

What this book does is to illustrate how some Shakespearean research that focuses on the text of the plays, but not to explain any play in terms of overall meaning for an audience, but rather, the autobiographical significance of specific passages, can be productive. Furthermore, I hope it will illustrate that we can give professional recognition to biographical research, often dismissed with the critical tag of "intentional fallacy," and perhaps suggest that a project to be encouraged in the future would be a scholarly Life of William Shakespeare to rescue him, rather than his plays, from obscurity. This endeavor attempts to begin the project with a few threads of play-text and life-text.

For the sake of focus I will restrict my data initially to a legal event in Shakespeare's life, and by no means exhaust its implications in the plays. We must not assume it was an overbearing preoccupation for Shakespeare's mind, although its effect is clearly traceable over a period of time. There were more important or more prevalent concerns, but what follows is both an example of the event as well as a suggested methodology that might elevate more of the text into the realm hitherto regarded as off-limit source material for a complete life. Simultaneously the life-text can begin to furnish clues of intentionality for some of the play-text. The event is a court case, a matter of record, and thus a conveniently authoritative source for biographical data. Furthermore that text can be easily used in conjunction with Shakespeare's generally acknowledged and widespread use of law language in his plays. Ultimately, then, Whitaker and Heilman's points will be confirmed, that a life of Shakespeare will conceivably offer some specific explanations about why certain passages, if not whole plays, were written the way they were and for what desired purpose. However, the scholarly ends or methods employed to obtain these results would not have been engaged in if the former writers' strictures had been followed. Finally life-text within outer horizons and play-text from within inner horizons may reach out to, or return to, their own contexts and produce a response that alters our perceptions of the whole matrix from which these texts came.

The literal case in point is that of *Shakespeare v. Lambert*, resulting from activity by Shakespeare's father, John, in 1578, and culminating in William's activities in Chancery, the highest court of the land, as late as 1599. Shakespeare did not refrain from references to his father's trade in his plays: he mentions his father's "glover's paring knife" in Merry Wives of Windsor (I.iv.21); his professional use of tanned hides and neat's leather in Hamlet (I.iv. 186-187) and Julius Caesar (I.i. 29); and dealings in wool in Winter's Tale as "Fifteen hundred shorn, what comes the wool to?" (IV.iii.35). Likewise in the tragedy that has presented us with the most dating and structural problems, *Timon of Athens*, we find in Timon's fate, a point-by-point description of Shakespeare's father's fall from civic height as mayor of Stratford, going into debt and bankruptcy, scorned by his ungrateful fellow citizens, being driven from public office, falling into a malevolent condition, and ending in an ignominious grave, as a result of his financial generosity and carelessness, finally refusing to leave his own house. All is borne out by public records and court testimony. The point is not that Shakespeare's *Timon of Athens* is an apologia for John by his son but it certainly is evidence against those who would say Shakespeare was unaffected artistically by, let alone unaware of, his father's financial and legal difficulties. And to follow Dr. Whitaker's recommendation one might find in this biographical research a possible explanation of why in *Timon*, most critics agree, Shakespeare's artistic judgment slips, flounders, and fails to achieve a successful tragedy.

As a result of John's financial difficulties in 1578, "the ebb of his estate and great flow of debts" (*Timon*. II.i. 150-151), he started to sell the rights in his wife's dowry and mortgage portions of his eldest, fourteen-year-old son William's inheritance from his mother. These developments are mirrored in Shakespeare's *Timon*:

> FLAVIUS.
> Though you hear now, too late -- yet now's a time --
> The greatest of your having lacks a half
> To pay your present debts.
> TIMON.
> Let all my land be sold.
> FLAVIUS.
> 'Tis all engag'd, some forfeited and gone;
> And what remains will hardly stop the mouth
> Of present dues: the future comes apace:
> What shall defend the interim? and at length
> How goes our reck'ning?
> TIMON.
> To Lacedaemon did my land extend.
> FLAVIUS.
> O my good lord, the world is but a word:
> Were it all yours to give it in a breath,
> How quickly were it gone! (II.ii. 152-163)

In debt to his importunate wool business; under suit from London for £30 in the Court of Common Pleas in Westminster; and being forgiven half his poor tax and any fines by the Aldermen in Stratford, John Shakespeare, in 1578, mortgaged Asbies Estate in Wilmcote outside Stratford to his brother-in-law's family, the Lamberts, for £40. Upon coming of age, William could have sustained himself on Asbies with its dwelling house and numerous acres of arable land. The engaged estate is to be forfeited if the £40 is not paid on Michaelmas Day, two years later. That, as it turns out, is only a year before William marries the pregnant Anne Hathaway, who recently inherited monies from her deceased father.

To defend the interim, and just before the due date, John sold more valuable rights in Snitterfield, ironically just before a mortally ill aunt succumbed, which would have made the ownership outright: "...she lingers my desires/Like to a step-dame or a dowager/Long withering out a young man's revenue." (*Midsummer Night's Dream*. I.i. 4-6). The Court of Queen's Bench levied such a fine on John for not attending court; it ate up his cash from the Snitterfield sale, leaving him with inadequate funds when the due date of his bond arrived in 1580. John offered his payment on Michaelmas, the due date for the bond to Edmund Lambert. He refused to accept. His acceptance, he says, will be upon the payment of all outstanding debts of John Shakespeare to him. Only oral agreements were made. The Shakespeares sought return of the estate upon proper payment through initial litigation in the Court of Record of Stratford; where, ironically, John Shakespeare had presided at his height as its Judge and High Bailiff. The Lamberts stood on the transfer, or alienation of title as a mortgage, becoming evidence of a sale upon the nonsatisfactory payment once the specific due date was technically passed without proof of extension or renegotiation. The upshot was the Lamberts, formerly Shakespeare family benefactors, an attitude evidenced by Mary and John naming William's brother "Edmund" after Lambert, Sr. during this interim, became enemies in court. Rather than relating to Shakespeare's youngest brother, this is why a thief of patrimony from a half-brother, (for Edmund was John Shakespeare's brother-in-law), in *King Lear* may have such negative associations and be named "Edmund." The Lamberts, Edmund, Joan and son John with Joan as Mary Arden Shakespeare's sister for whom Shakespeare's nonsurviving older and surviving younger sisters both were named, thereby retained Asbies upon forfeit from John, Mary and their son the dramatist William.

In 1587, assumed by many to be the beginning of Shakespeare's writing career, the Lamberts retain the Estate by inheritance as the lands, held by law, pass from old Edmund Lambert to his son, John, upon the former's death. Edmund's son now received the inheritance. Once crafty but now no longer quick, his son receives the inheritance once meant for William from his mother Mary's dowry. By this time William has reached his maturity and the Shakespeares, at a time when most scholarship mistakenly indicates there is an absolute blank in the dramatist's life-text, open the *Shakespeare v. Lambert* litigation in the Court of Queen's Bench in London, citing William as a party. This was at the time when John Shakespeare was not attending church, let alone civic or court sessions. Sometime between 1586 and 1592, most biographers think William came to London and conjectures about where he went and who set him up there abound. His family had an attorney in London, J. Stovall, who pursued the case in Westminster from the initial filing of the Complaint in 1588 until it was settled temporarily out of court in 1590.

This case was an attempt to regain mortgaged land by fine and recovery, a process punned upon twice in *Comedy of Errors* (II.ii. 73-75, IV.ii. 46-48), assumed to have been written around this time. The play is later to have its first public performance at one of London's leading law schools of Gray's Inn, December 28, 1594. The pursuit in court on the Shakespeares' part is verbatim that which Fortinbras articulates in *Hamlet* as he goes for lands so by his father lost (I.i. 86-95, 102-104) and at length in the Gravediggers scene (V.i.107-121). It was to the old Lambert's Cotswold dwelling in Barton-Upon-Heath John Shakespeare went on that Michaelmas Day, 1580, to redeem the property located in Wilmcote, outside Stratford. There is substantial indication of Shakespeare's concern about these matters, beyond the court record in his own plays, for in the Induction of *The Taming of the Shrew* he introduces "Christopher Sly, Old Sly's son from Burton-Heath" and "the fat ale-wife of Wincote." The Lamberts, like Sly, answered by law and would not budge an inch despite Shakespeare's attempts at remedy. The law-text thus can be seen penetrating the play's text and providing a basis for an interesting reading of the Induction and texts in other plays. Shakespeare's inheritance, then, has suffered a fate similar to that of Orlando's in *As You Like It*. It is being kept from him and his gentleman's state is being denied. This continues to rankle for many years as the person who was the cause of the forfeiture of the mortgage was none other than "Edmund". I leave it to my readers' responses to relate the fact from life-text to law-text and then to the play-text of *King Lear*, wherein Edmund, the half-brother of Edgar, steals his patrimony.

Between the end of the Shakespeares' litigation in Queen's Bench in 1590 and their reopening of it in Chancery in 1597, Shakespeare writes the trial scene in *Merchant of Venice* (IV.i.) depicting the failure of a lower court to provide remedy or equity with the Duke's powers strictly limited to upholding, not interpreting, laws.[12] The Lord Chancellor Sir Thomas Egerton, Lord Ellesmere, to whom Shakespeare's Chancery litigation is specifically addressed, subsequently informs King James on precisely this prudential point. If James failed to recognize the appellate and interpretive jurisdiction of Chancery "...you would be but the Duke of Venice."[13] Shakespeare's personal solution is to introduce Portia, providing, according to Chancery procedure, a merciful by an equitable, following the letter not just the intent, reading of the law-text within the play-text, thus obliterating Antonio's forfeiture on a bond. This was hopeful thinking on Shakespeare's part about his own losses by forfeiture on a bond; for within a year of the first recorded performance of the *Merchant*, the dramatist places himself in Chancery, England's court of equity and "gateway to Mercy".

This Chancery litigation, significant for legal history as well as Shakespearean biography, is seldom if ever mentioned and no identification of the attorneys, officers of the court, or the level to which the litigation reached has hitherto been made. We know Shakespeare is aware of the bifurcated court system of Chancery and Queen's Bench present in England at this time from his reference to a Judge of Equity in the mock trial scene of *King Lear*:

> KENT. Will you lie down and rest upon the cushions?
> LEAR. I'll see their trial first. Bring in the evidence.
> [To Edgar] Thou robed man of justice, take thy place;
> [To the fool.] And thou, his yoke-fellow of equity, Bench by his side.
> [To Kent.] You are o' the' commission,
> Sit you too.
> EDGAR. Let us deal justly. (III.vi. 36-42)

The Shakespeare Complaint is addressed directly to Thomas Egerton, Head of Chancery, and cites reasons of "equity" as well as justice and law for assigning the Asbies property to William Shakespeare. The witnesses called by the Shakespeares are all of William's, not his father's, generation. The expense of such litigation is considerably beyond his father's means, but not Shakespeare's, particularly at the level to which the case is going, coupled with the personages, besides the Lamberts and the Shakespeares, who become involved. On the Lamberts' side the attorney is Nicholas Overbury, the father of Sir Thomas Overbury. To match this Shakespeare retains two of the six Clerks of Chancery! These are Edward Huberd and Stephen Powle and act as William Shakespeare's attorneys. Stephen was the son, and at this time the Deputy of one of the four Masters of Chancery, Thomas Powle. The case itself finally went to one of the other Masters, John Hunt, Doctor of Laws, hitherto misidentified simply as "Mister D. Hunt". In 1599 the Shakespeares are finally denied remedy at the

Mastership level of England's superior court after being in the courts of Westminster on and off over a period of eleven years. Shakespeare must reconcile himself to the fact that the lands are so by his father forever lost.

A slight legal history addition to this study's text will complete the picture and give Shakespeare's attempts some vindication.[14] Although denied remedy in 1599, Chancery begins, just after the case, to recognize equity of redemption in mortgages and grace periods in loans as a direct result of the writings of the Masters in Chancery at this time. One of these Masters, who died in 1601, shortly after the completion of this case in his personal jurisdiction, was the great antiquarian and legal researcher for Sir Thomas Egerton, none other than William Lambarde. It was in private audience to William Lambarde in 1599 Queen Elizabeth made her only recorded reference to William Shakespeare and it was highly censorious; "Know ye not but I was Richard II and this tragedy was played forty times in open streets and house."[15] It was Lambarde who wrote in 1600 that no man should lose his estate upon a technicality; "...Chancery will compel the obligee to take his principal with some reasonable consideration of his damages." This is what Portia offered Shylock, but English law would not recognize at the time of writing and did by the repeated performance later before King James; "for if this was not, men would do that by covenant which they now do by bond..."[16] In his first paragraph of the remaining Master of Chancery's *Reports*, by George Carew (*Cary's Reports* ...out of the labours of Lambarde") not published until 1650 and therefore not seen as relating to Shakespeare's litigation and considerably postdating the exercise of the radically new practice in Chancery initiated by Lambarde. These connections between William Lambarde, who purchased tickets to Paris Garden performances during the time *Merchant of Venice* was on the boards there, who was overseeing Alienations in Chancery, and Shakespeare, whose case was one in which the alienation of land had taken place, are significantly meaningful with regard to their mutual interests. These connections spur current interest in the copy of Lambarde's *Archaionomia* in the Folger Shakespeare Library containing Shakespeare's autograph and a Westminster address: "...the authenticity of the signature has been widely discussed, and the weight of opinion now is that it is a genuine signature of Shakespeare". "That the two [Lambarde and Shakespeare] knew one another is not open to doubt."[17]

By tracing only briefly, identical phrasing in the plays, i.e. theater-text, and in the documents from law- and life-texts in the Public Records, evidence stands before us that Shakespeare wove personal legal moments from his life-text into his play-texts, especially in *The Taming of the Shrew* and *Hamlet*, allowing these to achieve direct intertextuality. Thereby an awareness of his life-text, previously so hermetically removed from his dramas, is necessary to fully comprehend what he is doing with his dramas' legal language, particularly in *Merchant of Venice*. This is an obvious play to focus on but no less crucial, as it turns out, are the results from similar investigations using these new approaches into *Measure for Measure* and *Twelfth Night*. Without ignoring the tragedies, it does appear Shakespeare seems to give freer rein to these concerns in the comedies. Perhaps histories allow for parallel concerns but not such overt references, and the tragedies, except for the problematic *Timon*, appear to stand freer, but not untouched thematically from, this preoccupation. Therefore it appears, except for *Hamlet* and *Lear* which have other overt connections with his family concerns and inheritance, the comedies, and particularly those designed to appeal to an exclusively legal audience at the Inns of Court, are the carriers of Shakespeare's personal struggle with his law case: *Comedy of Errors*, *Taming of the Shrew* and *Midsummer Night's Dream* in his early period; *Merchant of Venice*, *Twelfth Night*, and *As You Like It* at his artistic height; and *Measure for Measure*, *Winter's Tale* and *Tempest* in his position of power under King James. These will receive close attention.

One can see that there is much to work with in Shakespeare's life-text and the conjunction with play-text, intertext, constitutes a helpful confirmation of areas in which to disclose the author's presence, even intent. We can observe artistic transmutations as he reacts to his problems working themselves out. With considerable caution and judicious control, these moments of intertextuality can reveal autobiographical data. Furthermore, to the points by Virgil Whitaker and Robert Heilman, these approaches and findings can offer explanations for some of the dramatist's thematic preoccupations, their origins, and intended impact in several works. Can we continue to presume Shakespeare, who uniquely understood human life, would not have utilized in his portrayal of it events from his own life touching him most closely? The play-texts, as things, were not written in isolation and our analysis or use made of them need not be so either, unless supporting information or well-grounded methodology is absent.

Do not mistake what we are about to do as merely old nineteenth-century romantic criticism explicating *roman-a-clef* literature, seeking to explain by making concluding statements about the plays such as: *Timon of Athens* is a portrait of Shakespeare's father, *Merchant of Venice* is a personal criticism of an unjust legal system, or *King Lear* and the Induction of *The Taming of the Shrew* are vindictive satiric attacks on the Lamberts. The enterprise before us is both a much deeper, more personal investigation of how what is evidenced in *the life-text might give impetus and energy to the literary text*, which then begins to be governed by its generic and consequential production restraints and opportunities shaping the art from nature. It will also be an investigation of how the literary-text can through compensation reshape the context out of which the impulses originate. Gone then is the simplistic Aristotelian notion of art mirroring nature; this intertextuality flows in both directions, particularly when law plays are performed before a judicial audience. Shakespeare's experience in law influences his plays, which gain an intertextuality from law as their text enters the minds and speech of jurists of his day. Such conclusions must come from extremely subtle argumentation and close analysis of text qualified to indicate these connections are but one or two strands of many complex patterns working in Shakespeare's artifice. Even without overarching interpretive statements, however, this kind of research does result in major finds and connections, proving Shakespeare's personal connections with the law were lengthy, sustained, and at high levels of extremely important jurisdictions; therefore, we must regard his knowledge of law and the complexity of his use of it with more seriousness and certainly greater sophistication than we have previously. My purpose, in general, is to defend the multiplicity of approaches to Shakespearean research, and, more specifically, to plead for more scholarship, more writing and teaching in the realm of Shakespeare's biography and particularly as it can be related to the plays. Then our students, as they become devoted to the life of literary criticism, do not feel they are under some professional obligation to isolate his works from his life and therefore feel free to ignore the life out of which they all too evidently came.

We will now begin to look at the very beginning of Shakespeare's career in *Comedy of Errors*, and his first production at the Inns of Court. Here we will see life- and law-texts intersect with play-text. Later, in his more public dramas such as *Merchant of Venice* and *Twelfth Night*, we will witness his play-texts compensating for losses evidenced by his life- and law-texts. And finally, under King James, we will see how legal and dramatic language systems experienced and used by Shakespeare undergo a historical and personal crisis. They are seen to betray the masters of their use, failing to compensate, restore, or redeem, except to remain as substitute systems and enchanting "fictions".

Chapter II

Twins at the Inns of Court[1]

AEGEON	...she became A joyful mother of two goodly sons; And, which was strange, the one so like the other As could not be distinguish'd but by names. *Comedy of Errors.* I.i. 50-53
ANTIPHOLUS OF SYRACUSE	Farewell till then: I will go lose myself; And wander up and down to view the city.
FIRST MERCHANT	Sir, I commend you to your own content. [Exit]
ANTIPHOLUS OF SYRACUSE	He that commends me to mine own content Commends me to the thing I cannot get. I to the world am like a drop of water That in the ocean seeks another drop, Who, falling there to find his fellow forth, Unseen, inquisitive, confounds himself: So I, to find a mother and a brother, In quest of them, unhappy, lose myself. (ii. 30-39)

After marrying Anne Hathaway and the birth of Susanna in 1585, Shakespeare became the father of twins, christened with the names of the Shakespeares' next door neighbors who were the Sadler bakers — Judith and Hamlet (cf. previous chapter). That William Shakespeare should use "twinning", as in Cassius and Brutus, Laertes and Hamlet, Edgar and Edmund, and mistaken identity in *Measure for Measure* and *All's Well That Ends Well* is thereby not surprising. Source studies as well as biographical and psychological approaches can shed interesting light upon these recurrences. Yet more than of passing interest is the statistical significance and correlation of twins in Renaissance comedy and the performance of these plays at Inns of Court entertainments. Through the one fact of twins being used for comic purposes at the Inns, Shakespeare, the father of twins, can above all be noted. But he is seemingly also a fortuitous part of an hitherto unnoticed legal tradition including Marston, Gascoigne, Sackville, Norton, and Webster involving the law schools of Gray's Inn, Middle Temple, and Inner Temple Hall.

    There is no question that Shakespeare visited the Inns of Court on several occasions as he performed there in his own and Jonson's plays and witnessed several of his plays performed in their halls. In turn, the Inns of Court men clearly knew him through his acting, plays, sonnets, long narrative poems, court case, and personal stories about him. He knew of them as evidenced by references to specific Inns in his plays. Also his patrons, neighbors, relatives, and people he had transactions with were from these law schools. His cousin Thomas Greene from Stratford was in attendance while Shakespeare was writing in London. There are many reasons for a work to be found popular, enjoyable or attractive but I would like to suggest a specific reason why *Comedy of Errors* and later *Twelfth Night* were received with such interest, excitement, and praise at the Inns. Both of these plays, performed first before these schools, contain twins and this is not, I claim, any accident, particularly since an exclusively judicial audience is present.

Shakespeare himself would have also gone to the Inns of Court to talk over literature, translations, new styles of poetry, and plays, possibly borrowing books and manuscripts. He was doing first drafts of his plays, a practice he may have initiated in Stratford. He probably came to Westminster, where he had his family court case, and London with a manuscript of *Comedy of Errors* already in hand. This first draft, perhaps performed in school or amongst friends or pupils, was definitely revised for performance at the Inns of Court. It was selected for Gray's Inn's Christmas revels in 1594, a singular honor.

Comedy of Errors contains the sophisticated texture of a mercantile background with intertextuality from Roman law; and foregrounded from his life-text Shakespeare added complex arrest procedures and language from laws of debt from personal experience. The text contains knowledge of law-text in such particularities as earnest to bind or down payment (II.ii. 1-25). Of specific concern is the process by which Shakespeare in Queen's Bench has been attempting to reobtain Asbies once lost on a bond, now by fine and recovery - paying fees and having title returned. Recovery is a form of redemption by payment when there has not been a sale. Shakespeare puns on the process in his case twice in *Comedy of Errors*; as he will in *Hamlet*'s Gravedigger scene.

DROMIO.   There's not time for a man to recover his hair
             That grows bald by nature.
ANTIPHOLUS. May he not do it by fine and recovery?
DROMIO.   Yes, to pay a fine for a periwig and recover
             The lost hair of another man.
                                            (II.ii. 733-75)

DROMIO.   Will you send him, mistress, redemption,
             [Mistress Redemption]
             The money in his desk?
ADRIANA.   Go fetch it sister. This I wonder at, '
             That he, unknown to me, should be in debt.
                                            (IV.ii. 46-48)

Again, as in *Timon of Athens*, we have evidence of Shakespeare's knowledge of the particulars of his case. The old-style explication would leap into this intersection and extend the connection into purely surmise and conjecture — that he anticipated the lands would be "lost", that they were as vital to him as his hair, and/or that John's extensive debts were unknown to William until at least the date of the case. All that is clearly unwarranted. What does have warrant is the presence of the autobiographical references to "recover", "fine and recovery", "pay a fine", "recover", "lost", "another man", "redemption", "money" and "debt". What is connected from the case to the references in the play is a similar context of tone, an energy of anger over objects of purchase, transactions, debts and official charges. All this is mixed with confusion and false accusation involving twins.

Shakespeare shows off before a legal audience his knowledge of attachment and breach of promise (IV.i.); arrest upon meane process, "One that before the judgment carries poor souls to hell," "he is `rested on the case"; subornation and such exchanges as:

OFFICER.   He is my prisoner: if I let him go,
                The debt he owes will be requir'd of me.
                                        (IV.iv. 120-121)

ANTIPHOLUS.
      Fear me not, man; I will not break away.
      I'll give thee, ere I leave thee, so much money,
      To warrant thee, as I am `rested for.
                                          (II. 1-3)

The very language of law is captured in this dramatic text with the sounds of its colloquial and oral tradition. Shakespeare's first text and first private production is fraught with autobiographical content, or a text intertextualized with law-texts familiar to him and in his life-text. *Comedy of Errors* is about a father under bond missing his twin sons in a nonnative city with people being arrested and the threat of arrest for debt. These textual references appear straight out of Shakespeare's and his father's own personal experiences as can be seen in virtually any biographical account[2] but without, as usual, any connection being made to this play-text. Coinciding with the burlesque action is the concomitant release that it gave to the energy of anger accompanying his case.

By 1594, with his literary fame assured, particularly at places like the Inns of Court by his preeminently successful *Rape of Lucrece* (published May 9, 1594) and by having the Earl of Southampton as the acknowledged grateful patron of his work, access to dramatic presentation at Gray's Inn for Shakespeare would be easy to achieve. Possibly some of the members had seen previous works by Shakespeare commissioned by, and performed before, the Earl.

Shakespeare had in his first draft of *Comedy of Errors* a play, with its two sets of twins and resulting mistaken identity, that would be naturally popular for the inhabitants of Gray's Inn. The play is based on Plautus' *Menaechmi*, which had also influenced Ariosto's *I Suppositi*, being the source for another historical, literary event at Gray's Inn. A member of Gray's Inn, George Gascoigne, in 1566 wrote *Supposes*, based on Ariosto, being the first English comedy of distinction, and performed at Gray's Inn Hall. *Supposes* is used by Shakespeare as a source for his *Taming of the Shrew*. The plots of all these plays are based upon the existence of twins, disguised servants and role changes. These have particular appeal to lawyers, barristers, attorneys, and students of the Inns because when prosecuting according to English or Anglo-Saxon law, as opposed to Continental or Roman law, the defense only has to establish in the mind of the jury "reasonable doubt" as to guilt, since the presumption is the accused is innocent until proven guilty. In other words, the defense only has to put forth a substantial counter-hypothesis, all other things equal, producing the identical effect in the case by alternative means but ruling out their client as agent. Hence, any reality can result from hypothesizing identical results from different premises or causes. The case in comedy proves to be that of mistaken identity; thus the client, or supposed culprit, is declared innocent by virtue of their being the wrong "twin." One can easily see, then, that identical twins would cause attorneys legal and prosecuting nightmares as criminals or as inheritors to be punished or rewarded, found guilty or innocent. Accusing an identical twin of a sexual assault by witnesses, or even by victim, is fraught with evidential difficulty, and errors of that nature quickly get a case thrown out of court in the Anglo-American legal tradition.

We may wonder at Shakespeare's sensitivity to all these legal matters as a son of a debt-ridden glover, calf-skin, and wool merchant. We must not forget William was not apprenticed to a dealer in hides but rather had paternal influences from a Mayor, Chief-Alderman, High Bailiff, Sheriff and Judge of the Stratford Court of Record. John Shakespeare carried out much of the town's legal business. Shakespeare was the son of a magistrate deeply involved in numerous legal matters, and probably would have gone off to Oxford or Cambridge and on to the Inns of Court if his father had had any money.

Twice with *Comedy of Errors*, and once with *Twelfth Night*, the dates of performance are crucial indicators of further thematic associations. Prosecuting twins leads to mistaken identity and punishment of the innocent. A meaningful complement to the legal problems posed by twins exists in the fact that the several performances of *Comedy of Errors* in Shakespeare's lifetime, when it was done at the Inns in 1594 and much later again at Court in 1604, took place on Holy Innocents' Day, December 28th. This feast day celebrates the slaughter by Herod of the innocent children, among whom he hoped might be the Christ-child, an ironic example of fruitlessly trying to eliminate any chance of mistaken identity. Both performances before Elizabeth and James on the same date of Holy Innocents is beyond chance. Plays are linked to festive occasions and Holy Days. Whoever is head of revels presumes that *Comedy of Errors* and twins relates to the legal problem of determining and perceiving the innocent and avoiding mistaken identity. The festival day commemorates the fact there is only one Christ (no twins) and it is wrong for his mistaken "twins" to have suffered for their innocence by having been born around his time under Herod. What a mistake to kill the wrong twin!

The plot device of the twins was such an obviously repeatable success Shakespeare reproduces the basic premise in *Twelfth Night, or What You Will* for Middle Temple (February 2, 1602), which Manningham, a member of the Inns, in his diary says reminds him of Plautus' Menaechmi. John Marstson, a dramatist of Middle Temple law schools, was to get on the bandwagon too with his *What You Will* (c. 1601-1607), resembling *Twelfth Night* and *Comedy of Errors*.

Somehow, the *Comedy of Errors* was preferred. Someone like William Lambarde or John Donne who served in that capacity at Lincoln's Inn made the selection of the plays and entertainments for the Christmas revels at Gray's Inn. The famous revels at the Inn during the holiday season of 1594-95 were the most elaborate ever recorded. The series of events included a masque by Francis Davison, at least one poem written for the occasion by the famous Elizabethan poet and musician Thomas Campion, a group of speeches by Francis Bacon and Shakespeare's *Comedy of Errors*. The text of the revels survives and is entitled "*Gesta Grayorm*, or the History of the High and Mighty Prince Henry, Prince Purpoole....Who Reigned and Died, A.D. 1594. Together with a Masque as it was presented...for the Entertainment of Q. Elizabeth..." It was the custom to invite the Inner Temple law students to the revels at Gray's but it was so crowded that after attempting to be seated, and creating a hubbub with ritualistic rioting, the members of Inner Temple left. There was tilting, jousts, and vaulting and "...after such sports, a *Comedy of Errors* (like to Plautus his *Menaechmi*) was played by the players. So that night was begun and continued to the end in nothing but confusion and errors; whereupon it was afterwards called *The Night of Errors*."

Later a mock-arraignment was conducted to determine the cause of the mix-ups on the night when *The Comedy of Errors* was offered:

> ...the Prisoner was freed and pardoned, the Attorney, Solicitor, Master of the Request, and those that were acquainted with the Draught of the Petition (the invitation of the Inner Temple to Gray's Inn), were all of them commanded to the Tower; so the Lieutenant took charge of them. And this was the End of our Law-sports, concerning the Night of Errors.[3]

Shakespeare was part of an enormous mock legal ritual involving the Court, Inns of Court and courts wherein law students were trained in person, by text and by a moot court situation to acquaint themselves with the custom, language and procedure of high-level arraignments. Shakespeare's *Comedy of Errors* was a showcase for legal terms — an opportunity for students to laugh at their trade and Shakespeare to display his intertextual skill. It was a success, not one full of legal language system errors, for William. The play was embedded into the texture of an elaborate festivity including ritual rioting to culminate in the legal ritual of a trial, within which frame the boisterous and law language text of Shakespeare's was inserted.

In celebration of the newly restored friendship between Gray's and the Templars, a pageant was presented between December 9, 1594 and January 6, 1595, and those in attendance were the Right Honourable the Lord of the Great and Privy seals, Lord Ellesmere, Sir Thomas Egerton, to whom Shakespeare addresses his actual case, who had just managed to get his closest colleague, William Lambarde, appointed as one of his Masters of Chancery. Also in attendance was Shakespeare's patron of his narrative poems, the Earl of Southampton, and his friend, the Earl of Essex. In the audience, or participating in the processions were the Earls of Shrewsbury, Cumberland, Northumberland, and the Lords Buckhurst, i.e., Thomas Sackville of Inner Temple, one of the authors of *Gorboduc*, about twin claimants to the throne; Windsor, Mountjoy, Sheffield, Compton, Rich, Burghley, Mounteagle, and the Lord Thomas Howard; Sir Thomas Henneage and Sir Robert Cecil, with a great number of Knights and Ladies.[4]

In further support of legal interest in twins for presenting problems at law, *Gorboduc* may be cited. *Gorboduc*, or *Ferrex and Porrex* was the first English drama in iambic pentameter, and Shakespeare used it as a source for *King Lear*. It was performed in 1561, in Inner Temple Hall, and raised for Queen Elizabeth the question of what chaos would follow in selecting a nonexistent heir or one from twins, or two equal claimants. It was written by Inns of Court authors Sackville and Norton, the former in attendance at *Gesta Grayorum*. Queen Elizabeth, as she was for *Twelfth Night* and *Comedy of Errors*, was present at the performance of the text containing twins and law language pertaining to political issues, and this did not prevent her elevating one of the authors to a dukedom.

Shakespeare knew he would have such learned gentlemen as his judges, patrons, colleagues and auditors, so the text of *Comedy of Errors* was altered to include law-text to speak to such ears. On the occasion of this newest and most exciting opportunity for his play, the author adds to his earlier draft legal passages and two trial scenes appropriate to his specific audience. England had a system of jurisprudence chiefly associated with the high court of Chancery, headed at the time by Thomas Egerton, serving to supplement and remedy the limitations and inflexibility of the common law. Upon occasion, it functioned to provide extraordinary relief, payment in kind as opposed to damages, overriding justice coupled with what might appear to be mercy. This fount of equity was found only in Chancery, presided over by the Lord Chancellor or Keeper of the Great Seal and ruled by four Masters of Chancery, such as William Lambarde, author of *Archaionomia*, a copy of which in the Folger contains a Shakespeare signature, and his close associate George Carew of Middle Temple, 1586. This Sir George Carew, Carey of *Cary's Reports*, is neither the figure of the same name whose father, Lord Hunsdon, was the Lord Chamberlain and hence the patron of Lord Chamberlain's men. Nor is he the third figure of precisely the same name and station from Shakespeare's Stratford-upon-Avon, Lord Carew of Clopton, Earl of Totness. But undoubtedly all three, the friend of Lambarde, the son of Shakespeare's patron and the neighbor of Shakespeare, of these name-sakes knew each other at Court in London. The Lord Keeper, Egerton, attended *Gesta Grayorum* as did Sir Thomas Henneage, Master of the Rolls, the office later briefly assumed by William Lambarde before his death, at which appointment-interview the Queen made her remark about Shakespeare. Not only up-and-coming law students knew of Shakespeare's *Comedy of Errors*, but also the leading justices of the realm. The play-text not only contains intertextuality from law-text and life-text but was designed and altered for a significant legal context.

William West of Inner Temple wrote *Symboleography* on legal terms, and it was published in 1591, with revisions and additions again in 1594; possibly Shakespeare read it in manuscript in Inner Temple for a passage suggested by Leslie Hotson in *Love's Labour's Lost*. However, it is probable the dramatist added legal passages from Inns of Court writers, particularly William West, to his first drafts of *Love's Labour's Lost* and *Comedy of Errors* in 1594, both performed privately before members of Gray's Inn.

1594 marks a year in which several of Shakespeare's play-texts contribute to the then-current debate about the concept of equity coinciding with its appearance in law-texts in a number of treatises in print, being revised in manuscript. and in preparation. One of these was the highly influential William West's *Symboleography*, a word for the legal documents or instruments representing conveyance deeds, indentures, and the very law-textual matters of interest to Shakespeare and his case, done at Middle Temple Gate. He had added to it in this year of 1594, before *Comedy of Errors* was performed, "another Treatise of Equities, [on] the jurisdiction and proceedings of the high Court of Chauncerie." From time to time, West cites passages from Christopher St. Germain's *Doctor and Student*, a debate between a doctor of divinity and a student of laws so popular that an edition was published every few years since 1528. These texts were widely quoted and discussed. Furthermore, some of these editions were printed at Middle Temple, and we have evidence that these law-texts enter dramatic texts. Shakespeare's fellow dramatists Ben Jonson and John Marston read *Doctor and Student* as they take a word from the treatise and use it respectively in *Every Man Out of His Humour* (III.iv), dedicated to the Inns of Court, and *Satires* (III.viii), written in Marston's rooms in Middle Temple.

The word picked up, misspelling and all, is "synderesis." Marston writes "returne sacred Synteresis,/Inspire our trunches," and Jonson mocks it in a list of inkhorn terms as "the soules Synderisis." *Syntheresis* is Greek for the mystical bond between the body and the soul, the flesh and the spirit. In *Doctor and Student* it signifies the spark of life which *Equitie* (the bond) gives to the *Law* (the flesh) and *Justice* (the spirit of the law), making a living legal system out of the bare bones of the letter of the law. Again the bifurcated English system is adumbrated by justice being achieved by Chancery over Queen's Bench or Common Law. One can see even in the mixing of law-texts the opportunity for dramatic legal situations from play-texts. William West, quoting Christopher St. Germain's *Doctor and Student*, writes in his London 1594 edition:

> ...equitie may mitigate Rigorem iuris [rigorous justice], which equitie is no other thing, then [si.] an exception of the law of God, or of the law of reason, from the general principles of man's positive law, not agreeing

with them in some particularity, which exception is inwardly imployed
in every general ground or maxim of the Law.

(Section 29c)

In this passage can be seen the linguistic tension of today's wider
concern about the emerging friction between obtaining reasonable justice
in conflict with man's positive law. Exceptions prove God's law and
man's do not coincide; the legal language system is inadequate, except
when the law of reason uttered by an equitable judge corrects it. Equity
and Chancery allow for redemption, grace periods, and mercy in the
court. These problems are dramatized in the plays in the Inns of Court.

This concept of equity, or mercy, accommodating man's written laws
to human necessity is the introductory subject of the first scene in the
Comedy of Errors. The Duke of Ephesus, Solinus, explicates the legal
dilemma Aegeon, a merchant from Syracuse, is creating by entering
Ephesus: "I am not partial to infringe our laws, [your Duke having]
seal'd his rigorous statutes with their [i.e., Ephesians'] bloods,/Ex-
cludes all pity from our threatening looks./Therefore by law thou art
condemn'd to die." Aegeon pleads for equity from natural law
arguments: "...the world may witness that my end/Was wrought by
nature, not by vile offence,...", and feels his search for his wife and
twins led him into a "merciless predicament." The Duke speaks of the
conflict between his personal empathy and his official duty: "...we
may pity though not pardon thee."

> ...were it not against our laws,
> Against my crown, my oath, my dignity,
> Which princes, would they, may not disannul,
> My soul should sue as advocate for thee.
> But, though thou art adjudged to the death
> And passed sentence may not be recall'd
> But to our honour's great disparagement,
> yet I will favour thee in what I can.

(Cf. I.i. 4-150)

West goes on from the earlier passage to indicate clemency is only
proper to a Prince, one who legislates as well as judges. In *The Comedy
of Errors*, and later in *Merchant*, Shakespeare takes on the problem of
how a judge can dispense the law of reason (or God) when it would
violate man's positive law without destroying ("disannul") the
integrity of the legal language system.

The Duke grants Aegeon one day in which to obtain the thousand
marks ransom. Finally, in the last scene, Solinus is so moved by the
circumstances reuniting Aegeon with his twins, "against such odds

nature must have been a party", he refuses to accept the offer of even a few ducats. He has reason to abrogate the law in this extraordinary case:

ANTIPHOLUS
OF EPHESUS.
　　　　　These ducats pawn I for my father here.
DUKE.　　　It shall not need; thy father hath his life.

(V.i. 389-390)

It is of interest that the son is offering the money to redeem his father for a legal violation against literary convention and in keeping with Shakespeare's pursuits to compensate for his father's losses. The Duke is following West's important law-text:

> Wherefore in some cases it is necessary to leave the Words of the Law, and to follow that reason and Justice requireth and to that intent Equity is ordained; that is to say, to temper and mitigate the rigor of the law. (p. 53)

Shakespeare's *Comedy of Errors* intertextualizes his classical sources for the Inns of Court from various law-texts and dramatizes a crisis in law for a court of equity wherein the ruler suspends the law by taking the nature of the circumstances into consideration. His play-text is similar to the law-text in *Doctor of Divinity and Student of Law*, wherein the Roman Law (*lex scripta*) is mitigated by Christian theology in the play. Solinus (Solon representing the lawgiver) rules mercifully over the Ephesians, subjects of St. Paul's Epistle who must exercise spiritual law unto themselves.

During this *annus mirabilis* of producing plays for private performances and works for the nobility (*Venus and Adonis*, *Rape of Lucrece*, *Love's Labour's Lost*, and *Comedy of Errors*), Shakespeare is commissioned to do *A Midsummer Night's Dream* for a wedding in a great house. In *Comedy of Errors* he mentions twice the process by which he and others attempt recovery of estates, but at the very beginning of *Midsummer Night's Dream* he mentions his personal problem of having had his dowager aunt survive long enough to allow his father to eat up the rights before he could have the whole Snitterfield property.

> ...she lingers my desires,
> Like to a step-dame or a dowager
> Long withering out a young man's revenue.

(I.i. 4-6)

He is remembering something that occurred fifteen years earlier, but he would not have been physically between the litigation of Queen's Bench and Chancery at the time of this writing if it had not happened. The fact that this reference and those in *As You Like It*, *Hamlet*, *Taming of the Shrew* and other plays are so early and even more so in very initial positions in the drama give one pause: it is as if to warm up his pen he needed to get his blood flowing, and for that his personal loss leaps to mind. Clearly this reference, if beyond mere matter of fact, complains about intergenerational injustice with regard to supply or rights, and is certainly extended thematically through the play-text of *Midsummer Night's Dream*.

A number of arguments have been offered for the dating of 1594-1596 for the play's performance at a major wedding. Chief of these are the marriage of the third earl of Bedford to Lucy Harrington on December 12, 1594; that of the Earl of Derby to Elizabeth Vere, daughter of the Earl of Oxford, on January 26, 1595; or that of Rt. Hon. Thomas, son of Lord Berkeley, to Rt. Hon. Elizabeth, daughter of Sir George Carey, on February 19, 1596.[5] The Queen would have been present upon these occasions, and the latter wedding would have the further connection of including the son of the Sir Henry Carey, who was Shakespeare's players' patron until his death on July 23, 1596. Given these dates, the chances are high that the height of winter was the setting for the performance of *Midsummer Night's Dream* adds even more to its fictional charm.

For whichever of these noted weddings, Shakespeare once again has his text of *A Midsummer Night's Dream* address a noble audience, perhaps including judicial figures, and has his judicial personage engage in the same equitable and merciful action as the Duke of *Comedy of Errors*. He introduces, their identity confused, a pair of lovers. Duke Theseus toward the end of the play relinquishes "the sharp Athenian law" upon Hermia when he discovers the lovers in such concord in nature, even though his decision is against the will of her father. Early in his career the dramatist had obtained legal audiences for his texts and they were to witness his authority figures mitigate law-texts, to achieve justice upon twins or twin-like pairing in the plots.

This was to continue. We will analyze the blending of texts in detail later with remarkable personal implications in relationship to his own twins, but for our purposes in this chapter we want to complete the picture of his plays appropriately containing law-text for his Inns of Court audiences. With all his friends and relations from Stratford, such as the Marstons, the Greenes, the Combes, the Underhills, and

Humphrey Colles all situated at, or connected with, Middle Temple around 1602, it is not surprising to find Shakespeare overtly entertained and entertaining under the roof of its Great Hall, which he had already immortalized in *Henry VI Part One*, II.iv., the scene wherein he alters the historical text of the plucking of the white rose and the red initiating the Wars of the Roses to place it on familiar and highly complimentary ground:

LONDON, THE TEMPLE-GARDEN.

RICHARD. Great lords and gentlemen, what means this silence?

PLANTAGENET. Dare no man answer in a case of truth?

SUFFOLK. Within the Temple-hall we were too loud;
The garden here is more convenient.

PLANTAGENET. Then say at once if I maintained the truth;
Or else was wrangling Somerset in the error?

SUFFOLK. Faith, I have been truant in the law,
And never yet could frame my will to it;
And therefore frame the law unto my will.

SOMERSET. Judge you, my Lord of Warwick, then between us.

(II.iv. 1-10)

This text bespeaks of the law not satisfying "will" and so having "will" frame the law.

Will, this son of Warwick, put on a *Twelfth Night* that kept them laughing in Temple Hall. The diarist John Manningham of Middle Temple records a performance before his society on Candlemas Day, 1602:

> February 2, 1602 - At our feast wee had a play called "Twelve Night, or What you Will," much like the Commedy of Errores, or Menechmi in Plautus, but most like and neere to that in Italian called *Inganni*. A good practice in it to make the Steward beleeve his Lady widdowe was in love with him, by counterfeyting a letter as from his Lady in generall termes, telling him what shee liked best in him, and prescribing his gesture in smiling, his apparaile, etc., and then when he came to practice making him beleeve they tooke him to be mad.[6]

Manningham caught Shakespeare's popular device of the twins from the earlier plays: *Twelfth Night* was almost a "What! You, Will, again!" Queen Elizabeth, had seen *Comedy of Errors* performed in 1594 before being performed at Gray's Inn as produced for Queen Elizabeth at Greenwich, so in 1602 she saw *Twelfth Night* at Whitehall before it appeared at Middle Temple. All the plays of Shakespeare that the Queen saw were comedies: *Comedy of Errors*, *A Midsummer Night's Dream*, *Merry Wives of Windsor*, and *Twelfth Night*, all in different locations during her reign. In addition to the sure-fired plot, the jokes, and the great songs ("O mistress mine, where are you roaming?" II.iii; "Come away, come away, death." II.iv; "When that I was and a little tiny boy,/With hey, ho, the wind and the rain..." V.i.) and other snatches, Shakespeare intertextualizes his play for his Inn's audience. The text is replete with references to exceptions and modest limits of order, proof, argument based upon admission against interest (I.v. 69-78); misprison, Sheriff's post, from which comes the Deed Pole, where indentures were posted for public announcements, misdemeanor, grand jury, "...you keep o' the windy side of the law..." (III.iv.); action of battery; and being "both the plaintiff and the judge/Of thine own cause." (V.i.).7 Many of these references are from William's concerns, "exceptions"; his father's experience and offices, "Sheriff's post"; and William West's treatise, "proof"; and St. Germain's "nonself-incriminating evidence."

By the time he writes *Twelfth Night*, performed later in Middle Temple, Shakespeare's lengthy case has only just been dismissed from Chancery in 1599, he has appealed to conscience in *Merchant of Venice*, and has encountered Masters and Clerks of Chancery. This indicates that Shakespeare's relationship with Chancery, equity, the Lord Keeper, Chancellor, William Lambarde and other writers of law-texts and the Inns of Court was a continuing one, from his case in 1588 to *Comedy of Errors* in 1594 and onto 1602. William had extended the period of his commitment to performing plays before a juristic audience, using a legal vocabulary in his plays, pursuing litigations in Westminster, reading the law writers and being involved in extending the text concerning the theory and practice of equity, which he had initiated from 1588 to 1594.

So Shakespeare, father of twins, was involved through his comedies with twins at the Inns of Court and was also part of a much larger legal tradition of twins in drama before juristic audiences. These were *Gorboduc* (1561) in Inner Temple, *Supposses* (1566) in Gray's Inn, based upon Ariosto and Plautus and Terence, *Taming of the Shrew*, *Comedy of Errors* (1594) Gray's Inn, *Twelfth Night: or What You Will* (1602) Middle Temple Hall, and *What you Will* by Marston of Middle Temple. Webster's *Duchess of Malfi* has twins. This leads to the biographical, historic and intertextual conclusions that in writing, selecting and producing these plays the authors, translators, actors and juristic audience were aware of the particular interest lawyers have in the legal nightmare offered by mistaken identity in the English judicial system. So the comedies are about identity, what one is responsible for, or innocent of, and above all what Shakespeare had an opportunity to observe in his own twins -- what made the differences in personality and gender from rural and noble backgrounds as he gentled his condition through his craft, money, knowledge, and contact with the aristocracy. Most important, he grew in the awareness of the complexity and ability inherent in law language. Not performed at the Inns of Court, but very much a text coming from the same literary sources as *Comedy of Errors* (even more emphatically from his law case) is *Taming of the Shrew*. An earlier version of this attacked lawyers, but Shakespeare's final version removes the satire and makes jurists argue more as friends. We now can assume that Shakespeare not only introduced his life-text into his play-text but also that his texts are firmly a part of a context at the Inns of Court.

The intersection of the court case and *Taming of the Shrew* allows another level of inquiry to be explored. Formerly we could only deal with elements within the text known as New Criticism, or earlier only subjective, personal aesthetic opinions. Northrup Frye allowed New Criticism to take *explication du texts*'s discoveries of repetitive mini-structures and extrapolate from them to analogous generic texts in *Anatomy of Criticism*.[8] This led us to welcome intertextuality, on the one hand with structuralism and literary archetypes, on the other. C. L. Barber, through close examination of the text of particular Shakespearean comedies, discovered the presence of elements outside classical literature in *Shakespeare's Festive Comedy*. This led to the necessity of extratextuality in criticism. The creativity of criticism did not stop there. Myth, archetypes, and the discovery of other texts were foregrounded or backgrounded in literature from religion, law, medicine, politics, philosophy, science, history, biography, autobiography and life-texts (by O. B. Hardison, Richard Shoecke, Linda Voigts, David M. Bergeron, Sherman Hawkins, Roy W. Battenhouse, M. W. Tilliard, Coppelia Kahn, Mary Ellen Lamb, Sam Schoenbaum and many others). But the direct effect of breaking from a pristine, hermetic and irrelevant text had been made by Frye's leap from one text to all other "literary" texts. Barber's move from a text out to social festival customs, as we saw at the Inns of Court, and structures with the creative release toward clarification of an individual artist looked backward for one moment. One can see how this might apply to Shakespeare's reversal of his personal notions and court case in comedies. That moment is when the artist introduces his, or her, structured linguistic, or gestured response to what otherwise are the structures imposed by the culture. If Frye leads us from Jung, then Barber leads us from Freud. I use the word "from" deliberately, the reverse of "to." We do not have to postulate the collective unconscious, nor the id; we only have a text, but a text greatly expanded into the realm of all writing, language, symbol systems, gestures, acts, silences and human activities, forming a coherent web. If we agree to find it in our criticism, from, say, the Boy bishop to Falstaff, from the seasons to genre, from New Comedy to Romance, from the Greek tragedies to "Never on Sunday," from King Arthur to "Star Wars", and from Shakespeare's comedy to his very life-concerns we will begin to practice a truly comprehensive kind of criticism.

All of Shakespeare's comedies, according to Frye, are related, or form a continuum structurally, and by Barber's lights a number of them are explicitly festive, or imbued with not just pastoral elements but moments mirroring social release. When performed, these have a cathartic release akin to tragedy, wherein audiences' responses are gathered into an attack on a cultural convention, vented in release, from which social conventions, beliefs emerge: such as gender in *Twelfth Night*, identity in *Comedy of Errors*, humanity in *Merchant of Venice*, loyalty in *All's Well That Ends Well*, nature of imagination in *Midsummer Night's Dream*. These are social transactions; symbiotic personal ones can also be taking place with regard to death, twins, financial losses, and inheritance. We will also look at three significantly placed comedies in relationship to Shakespeare's life and legal encounters revealing a development in his dramatic relationship to his autobiographical material: *The Taming of the Shrew*, *As You Like It*, and *Measure for Measure*. Are the respective main personalities of the first satirized, next adored, and last scorned, all out of measure by their creator in these still somewhat enigmatic plays to be successfully accommodated by the genre, or explained merely by the social creative impulse? Must we, if we can, reach beyond prototype and archetype, genre and custom to the origins of these by finding some link to Shakespeare's shaping impetus? Of course he had sources; of course the language quickly developed its own rules; of course language comes from nothing and returns to nothing, but before it vanishes are there brief exhalations coming from Shakespeare's life-text that suggest why he uttered this, this way, and at that time? As C. L. Barber knew and Virginia Woolf said, "...Shakespeare's plays...are the work of suffering human beings attached to...health and money and the houses we live in" (cf. previous chapter).

As we look at this development level of the phenomenon now in *The Taming of the Shrew, As You Like It* in the next chapter, and *Measure for Measure* in the following, I would like to specifically point to the preoccupation we have been exploring in each text that relates to the experience recorded in Shakespeare's life-text. The moments are divided into a sequence of episodes relating to Shakespeare's court case, first in Stratford, then in Court of Queen's Bench, and finally in Chancery. There may be a congruence between the tone or attitude, perceived by Frye and Barber, in each play, and Shakespeare's changing attitude toward his own court case. If, indeed, that is so and that the nature of the micro-play coincides with the micro-autobiographical element, the autobiographical moment or impetus, as C. L. Barber so elegantly suggests,[9] might be driving the shape of the play within its usual generic conventions. This point is crucial to this book and cannot be overemphasized. It might address the very thing "intentional fallacy" avoided and has been universally denied Shakespeare because of the avoidance of biography, let alone recognition of autobiographical elements or dimensions.

A literary work may be ordered: "Show me Falstaff in love" said Queen Elizabeth; it may fulfill generic conventions—revenge heroes do not survive their play; it may be influenced by its production as is Milton's epic and the lengthy *Hamlet*; and it may adhere to its sources, as *Antony and Cleopatra* does in regard to Plutarch. But a work, even in Russia, contains the seed of the author's choice and the impetus of concern and attitude toward an autobiographical event, however small a presence in the text. Read Virginia Woolf, listen to John Updike on his novels on the Kennedy assassination or Vietnam War in *Couples* discussed in *Paris Review*,[10] Spenser and Book V of *The Faerie Queene*,[11] Mozart's "mio padre" in *Don Giovanni*, etc. Knowing this does not make the art less and may make it also far more interesting. The audiences, in fact, knew about Shakespeare's case and those listening to Mozart's operas in his lifetime included those who were as aware of their autobiographical content as are today's nonacademic audiences who know it from *Amadeus*, the play or film.

Furthermore in Shakespeare, once we accept these conjunctions, other exciting things may follow. Since law is a language system independent of everyday, on the one hand, and literary speech patterns, on the other, we may be witnessing a conjunction or working out of one language system's frustration by giving vent to it in an analogous, or intersecting, system via intertextuality. In other words from our particular example: personal judgment ("I want my father's land back"), becomes courtroom drama ("lands lie in John Lambert's lawful possession by inheritance from his father"), and finally theatrical text ("Lands so by his father lost and to him all his lands restored"). When seeking justice becomes justice denied, perhaps it culminates in the artistic fulfilling of one's self-justifications.

Both Frye and Barber suggest *Taming of the Shrew* is a comedy requiring justification and explanation. It is at odds and in considerable tension with its form.[12] The audience in, and outside the play, has to be reconciled to these new characters who burst their stereotypical *commedia del arte* roles. The characters are not collapsed back into their roles; rather the nature of the revealed personalities of Kate and Petruchio, destroying conventions willy-nilly, raise attitudes striking out at conventionality with anger, questioning, and ultimate irresolution. Frye observes:

> The banquet at the end of *The Taming of the Shrew* has an ancestry that goes back to Greek Middle Comedy; in Plautus the audience is sometimes jocosely invited to an imaginary banquet afterwards; Old Comedy, like the modern Christmas pantomime, was more generous, and occasionally threw bits of food to the audience. As the final society reached by comedy is the one that the audience has recognized all along to be the proper and desireable state of affairs, an act of communion with the audience is in order.
>
> *Anatomy of Criticism*, p. 164

Kate and Petruchio have vented so much anger and hostility on one another that their respective stereotypes of docile wife and protective husband have been destroyed and made unbelievable; their characters as independent, unconventional and strong people emerge as worthy adversaries. Likewise, Barber notes Christopher Sly has the right genre but not the right content:

> When the bemused tinker Sly is asked with mock ceremony whether he will hear a comedy to 'frame your mind to mirth and merriment,' his response reflects his ignorant notion that a comedy is some sort of holiday game -- 'a Christmas gambold or a tumbling trick.' He is corrected with: 'it is more pleasing stuff...a kind of history.' Shakespeare is neither primitive nor primitivist; he enjoys making game of the inadequacy of Sly's notions of entertainment. But folk attitudes and motifs are still present, as a matter of course, in the dramatist's cultivated work, so that even Sly is not entirely off the mark about comedy. Though it is a kind of history, it is the kind that frames the mind to mirth. So it functions like a Christmas gambol.
>
> *Shakespeare's Festive Comedy*, p. 12

But off the mark Sly is, with genre correct, but content far more upsetting than mere fun-filled play. Sly is not only drunk, but also wrong, simple, and being made fun of. There are too many real issues here to be a mere game.

Christopher Sly, son of Old Sly, is from Barton-upon-Heath ("Burton Heath"), drinks with the Alewife from Wilmcote ("Wincote"), and when the Hostess goes for remedy against his drunkenness, by fetching the constable, Sly says: "Third, or fourth, or fifth borough, I'll answer him by law, I'll not budge an inch, boy: let him come and kindly" (*Induction*). This passage of exchange contains *four* references to Shakespeare's court case: *Old* Edmund Lambert's son John, from *Barton-on-the-Heath* in the Cotswolds would not return Shakespeare's mortgaged inheritance situated in *Wilmcote* on the grounds of a *legal* technicality (rather than the clear intent to pay) of not receiving the payment on the prescribed day. This was argued before the Court of Record in Stratford earlier and again 1588-90 in Court of Queen's Bench in Westminster. Shakespeare did as Tranio says, "...do as adversaries do in law,/Strive mightily,..." Shakespeare was angry and strove mightily against his adversary as the legal documents reveal, even within their conventionality. He is chided by the court for filing *two* Bills of Complaint against the Lamberts. Within those forms Shakespeare attempted to quell his adversary and conquer his discontent. He did not contain his unrest or find resolution within the bounds and went, after *Taming of the Shrew* and during the time of *As You Like It*, to Chancery on appeals upon losing judgment on the bond, which he, of course, is attempting to win in fiction through Portia in *Merchant of Venice*.

Shakespeare clearly borrows his experience from his personal case and inserts it into *Comedy of Errors* for a lawyer audience. As a father of twins, he cannot help but reinforce and give natural wit to his contribution to the twins in the dramatic tradition at the Inns of Court. His encounter with law and dramatization of justice and equity is in keeping with the intellectual theory and judicial texts of the very moment and place he is writing and where his work is being performed. Life-text, law-texts, and play-texts are obviously interlaced at psychological moments of crisis, anger, and disappointment, compensating for or reobtaining his father's losses. The references to his recalcitrant uncle and loss of his patrimonial properties obviously rankle explicitly in the Induction of the *Taming of the Shrew*. We see, then, the presence of the case, law, and twins in initial positioning of opening scenes in the play texts. Equity and attempts to compensate for the father and mercy and forgiveness are resolved in the dramas' final scenes. But much of the interim is boisterous, full of anger, confusion and injustice, straining the genre's forms. Shakespeare's life offers material for his own dramatic consideration and attitudes can be discerned in tone and judicial figures; furthermore judgmental situations force solutions upon circumstances straining against the ordinary. But even here these ends are wished for and obtained by the characters by special dispensation. Shakespeare is not quite yet asking for dramatic fiction to give him the solutions life does not.

Chapter III

A Son's Loss and Compensation[1]

OLD GOBBO.
> Can you tell me whether one Launcelot that dwells with him, dwell with him or us?

LAUNCELOT.
> Talk you of young Master Launcelot? [Aside] Mark me now; now will I raise the waters. Talk you of young Master Launcelot?

OLD GOBBO.
> No, master, sir, but a poor man's son: his father, though I say it, is an honest exceeding poor man and, God be thanked, well to live.

LAUNCELOT.
> Well, let his father be what a' will, we talk of young Master Launcelot.

OLD GOBBO.
> Your worship's friend and Launcelot, sir.

LAUNCELOT.
> But I pray you, ergo, old man, ergo, I beseech you, talk you of young Master Launcelot?

OLD GOBBO.
> Of Launcelot, an't please your mastership.

LAUNCELOT.
> Ergo, Master Launcelot. Talk not of Master Launcelot, father; for the young gentleman, according to Fates and Destinies and such odd sayings, the Sisters Three and such branches of learning, is indeed deceased, or as you, would say in plain terms, is gone to heaven.

OLD GOBBO.
> Marry, God forbid! the boy was the very staff of my age, my very prop.

LAUNCELOT.
> Do I look like a cudgel or a hovel-post, a staff or a prop? Do you know me, father?

OLD GOBBO.
> Alack the day, I know you not, young gentleman: but, I pray you, tell me, is my boy, God rest his soul, alive or dead?
>
> *Merchant of Venice* II.ii 49-75

Although *Comedy of Errors* has a twin seeking to redeem his father and Christopher Sly is to be converted to a benign, rewarded audience by being presented elaborate fictional art, these are not essential nor sustained elements of the plots. By the time he does lose his own son and is monetarily recouping his own father's losses, Shakespeare does turn to his drama to compensate losses and provide the wish-fulfillment he needs for these personal crises evidenced from the life-text. The play-texts that most clearly evidence these elements and substitute for specific losses in his case and in his son are *Merchant of Venice* and *Twelfth Night,* also involving law and the Inns of Court.

38

By the time of *Merchant of Venice*, Shakespeare is not only trying to get an estate back he lost that his only son would have inherited, but he has now lost the son.

> GOBBO.   Alack the day, I know you not, young gentleman, but I pray
>   you tell me, is my boy, God rest his soul, alive or dead?
>
> (II.ii. 70-72)

Gobbo is only one of many fathers in *Merchant of Venice* concerned about their offspring and their inherited wealth. Launcelot Gobbo has "an honest exceeding poor man and, God be thanked, well to live as a father." Jessica's father is distraught over "My daughter! O my ducats! O my daughter." Portia's father's clever will has devised the lottery of the three caskets and Antonio also plays the beneficent, sacrificing father-figure to Bassanio's "prodigal" (I.i. 129) son. Each offspring in varying degrees from Portia to Jessica chafe at these ties among flesh and blood that bind: Portia says it is hard to be curbed by such a will (I.i. 25); Bassanio has "...disabled mine estate,/by something showing a more swelling port/Than my faint means would grant continuance" (I.i. 123-25); Launcelot, the only actual son in the play, pretends he is dead to his father; and Jessica acts in such a way Shylock wishes she were dead. The closeness of these younger generations to the older is in almost direct proportion to the amount of wealth the elders have, can, or are willing to transfer to them. Granted, the *Merchant of Venice* is about much else too but the text certainly contains a deep concern for the tenuous legal means for successful transfer of estates from one generation to another. In fact this is what we have been observing all along - Shakespeare's growing awareness of the continuity in passing estates from one generation to another. This is an "aristocratic" awareness and in keeping with Shakespeare's striving for landed gentry status. These accumulations were denied by the Lambert's interfering with his inheritance from his mother; his father's dissipation of his estate; he knew he would have to acquire for his family, including a son; and then he would lose the unity of his estate with it going to two daughters upon the death of his Hamlet.

In light of these preoccupations of *Merchant of Venice* with offspring, inheritance, wills, dowries, generation of income, houses, estates, accumulated wealth and the laws of property preserving these rights, I would like to suggest we glance at Shakespeare's life-text at the time of the writing, particularly since we do not have direct literary sources for this play of numerous popular plots. What was Shakespeare's close family situation around 1596-1598 during which time the play is believed to have been composed? We can assume many things happened to Shakespeare during this period and have been lost to history. It is something of an exaggeration to rely on the good fortune of legal and church records. However this play and others are informed by legal concepts; and we can assume a first family death for Shakespeare, the survivors, and traumas in his immediate family did not go without impact upon his creative imagination. And like the very beginnings of *Comedy of Errors, A Midsummer Night's Dream, Taming of the Shrew, Twelfth Night* and *As You Like It*, Shakespeare has *Merchant of Venice* begin with the later recipients of good fortune in despair:

> ANTONIO. In sooth I know not why I am so sad.
> It wearies me, You say it wearies you;
> But how I caught it, found it, or came by it,
> What stuff 'tis made of, whereof it is born,
> I am to learn; [sigh]
> And such a want-wit sadness makes of me
> That I have much ado to know myself.

(I.i. 1-7)

This may be a comedy and merry old England but there was much, as we know, at this time to cause Shakespeare sadness and concern. His father, we remember what happened to John, had vaulted into his position of Mayor or High Bailiff of Stratford and, in a process analogous to what Shakespeare traces for *Timon of Athens*, loaned out money to his friends with similar dreadful results. He had been prosperous as a glover, dressing leather and dealing in wool, the mercantile and artistic side of rather pastoral products. As first citizen of Stratford, a position of considerable significance in such a key trading town, he presided over cases of debt, sealed leases, looked after town lands and investments. At his height he was "...leasing meadows from the former Clopton estate, and in October 1575 he bought two more houses with gardens and orchards, in the town for £40; and before that he "had stood surety for an acquaintance at Shottery, Richard Hathaway, for two debts which were paid when harvest came in."[2] As Honigman suggests, John Shakespeare, himself, was a money lender.[3] John's confidence was such that in 1575-76 he started to apply to Herald's College for a grant of a coat of arms. This application is dropped and only renewed by Shakespeare the son on behalf of his poor father October 20, 1596 around the time he writes of poor Gobbo constantly referring proudly but mistakenly to his son Launcelot as *Master* Launcelot (II.ii. 33-72).

These details are in the Estate Records for Shakespeare's father going into sudden and painful social, economic, legal and religious decline from 1577 until his death in 1601, wherein he does not leave his house for fear of arrest, definitely for debt, probably money lending with interest, and possibly recusancy. During this time Shakespeare's inheritance of Asbies Estate from his mother's Catholic parents, the Ardens, is mortgaged on a bond to his Uncle Edmund Lambert and, as we have noted, John fails payment two years later; alienated in 1578, due 1580. Queen's Bench gets the *Shakespeare v. Lambert* case, to get the loan on a bond back, from 1588to 1590 but it is rejected. Shakespeare is attempting to recoup his father's losses. Shakespeare, coinciding with his resubmission for the Coat of Arms search, seeks to win the case again in Chancery beginning November 24, 1597. Shakespeare is to have no inheritance, save the birthplace residence and perhaps business debts but probably their interest from his father; he has seen his father lose several estates and his inheritance he was to receive from his mother. He has lost a case upon a bond and sees it fall to the use of his uncle. He has a family of Anne, his eldest Susanna, and his twins Hamlet and Judith to support. His son would inherit. He must eventually find a good house reflecting his expectations. So he purchases on May 4, 1597 New Place, brick and the largest residence in town, so he has income or equity if these are not built on sand.

The Fates and Destinies (II.ii. 62-63) have been against him. His only son and heir dies at the age of eleven on August 11, 1596;

> Upon my head they placed a fruitless crown
> And put a barren scepter in my grip,
> Thence to be wrenched with an unlineal hand
> No son of mine succeeding
>
> Macbeth III.i. 62-65

Subsequently, after his purchase of New Place from Hercules Underhill, he discovers the transaction is undermined by the fact the two-faced gentleman poisoned his father, Underhill, Sr. in order to inherit: "...murder cannot be hid long - a man's son may,..." (*Merchant of Venice*. II.ii. 79-80). His house, a major residence, might go to the State (cf. IV.i. 370-375). Even Shakespeare's own gentle craft and thereby income is subject to legal attack at this time from October 9 to November 29, 1596, when there is action to close down Paris Garden.[4]

Let me review Shakespeare's life-text, a moment, at the time of the creation of his play-text and note some surprising implications beyond mere parallels. These raise beyond a relationship to his case and personal losses a question of viewpoint toward characters in the play, an attitude toward law language and the function play-text can have to life-text. Shakespeare's father is a recluse now and possibly because of the wrong religion and, definitely because in extreme debt, or due to illegal transactions, confined to his house. Shakespeare's livelihood has been attacked with threatened removal. His major property might go to the State. He has lost his heir. His inheritances from both his mother and his father are being foregone. And his court case, on failure to pay a debt on a bond, is being lost. Who is losing all this in *Merchant of Venice*? Shylock! This biographical text becoming autobiographical text in the play should come as a considerable surprise, perhaps some of these possessions were worth a wilderness of monkeys to William, as we do have evidence he methodically works to gain back all his father lost; "Alack, what a heinous sin is it in me/To be ashamed to be my father's child!" (II.iii. 16-17). Is the solution to problems in *Merchant of Venice* to suddenly find Shakespeare "is" Shylock? Or that Shakespeare's father is being depicted in Shylock? No! But by now when we read the court case in *Merchant of Venice* and know the one from Shakespeare's life-text is being referred to in *Taming of the Shrew* and *Lear* with Barton-upon-Heath, Wilmcote and Edmund, we, perhaps, can broaden our sense of "sources" to include the biography for the resulting play-text of the period. Perhaps the first seeing of a play need not be colored by this knowledge but when members of audiences see several plays and the same one on many occasions, and in different versions, it is not inappropriate for them as a result of a quick read of a biography, to watch themselves discover or even see instantly how autobiographical aspects of them are. In fact it is quite natural and we do it with every Spielberg or Fellini film without even reading their biographies.

When we note autobiographical elements in Shakespeare resonances follow, particularly as the play refers to ventures and losses in England, to Medea who killed her children but renewed Jason's father; to lambs and fleeces; to land in third use by an uncle (I.iii. 68-90) and of course the debts. The authorial concern and manipulation of plot appears to be to protect inheritance by a) deed of gift to Jessica and by b) having Portia's inheritance pass successfully to Bassanio in the form of a house and wealth, specifically that which is being withdrawn from the author in his life-text as he is writing the play-text. Some of this crosses over explicitly: Hercules Underhill is the figure who killed his father for his inheritance, which Shakespeare purchases:

> There is no vice so simple but assumes
> Some mark of virtue on his outward parts.
> How many cowards whose hearts are all as false
> As stairs of sand, wear yet upon their chins
> The beards of Hercules...
> To be the dowry of a second head,
> The skull that bred them in the sepulcher.
>
> (III.ii. 81-85, 95, 96)

We cannot say when these analogies come to him in relationship to the events nor to his writing -- he, like us, may only notice after it appears in the text before him. We cannot be so subtle as to pin it down. The plays and the allusions are public, and Underhill may not have had a beard, but the allusions to us and to Shakespeare that the text provides cannot, before or after the fact, elude him and therefore need not us. Shakespeare, like Shylock with no son; holds, like the play, a barren estate and fruitless inheritance as far as continuation of his last name. He must now, as in the drama, pass it on, not entire, but by dividing in half for the unknown husbands-to-be of his two remaining daughters. By the unfortunate laws of the time, that generation no doubt raced to have the first son to inherit all as do Nerissa and Portia (III.ii. 213).

So if Jessica is not Shakespeare's lost son, or Shylock Shakespeare's father, where do these bio-data and play-text conjunctions lead us. I think to something far more subtle and interesting. Shakespeare experiences these losses in his life, as we have seen, of inheritance and offspring so he knows what risks and chance exist. He knows that law can prevent loss, furnish compensation and reward, as can an equally subtle language system by displacement known as the art of dramatic fiction. He has lost his case by common law and goes to Chancery, a Court of Equity -- the gateway of mercy -- and goes at the same time to the public bar of the theater boards and through fiction and verbal trickery wins his case. Shakespeare has Antonio win in the play a similar case to what Shakespeare is losing in reality in his own life. On the other hand, Shylock by losing the case in the play is experiencing, thereby, losses similar to what Shakespeare's father and family are suffering. The romance in this comedy is that the "beneficent" father-figures bestow their goods on the two daughters (Portia and Jessica), the two sons-in-law (Bassanio and Lorenzo), and the pretended dead son (Launcelot) by the workings of the law in the play through "mercy" (equity). The inheritances, estates, house, sons through marriage (III.ii. 213), lead a father to Christian salvation through forced conversion, and the renewing of "old" men is achieved by this comic main plot. This is clearly in all its details wish-fulfillment for many of Shakespeare's own similar actual losses only allowed to be threatening in the play. This artistic energy we witness itself sustains Shakespeare into repurchasing the house, reopening the case, buying back lands his father lost, to go on to write a play named for his dead son Hamlet and engage in building the Globe. That does not, however, address the moment in 1597 when *Merchant of Venice* results in a "dark" comedy, a sick Shylock, a bad taste in our mouths, and on such a night remembering Cressid was false; Pyramis killed himself, as did Dido; and Medea killed her children. All were cut off from their other half, or heroic beginnings by war, mischance, duty and alienating society.

Shakespeare does make his plot work toward a comic resolution with magnificent acquisitions, marriages and the fulfilling of inheritance and promise of sons. Not Mercy and no "grace period" nor "equity of redemption" but rather a *precise reading of the word* (letter) of the law and revealing its strictest limits of intent wins the case. This is a key personal vision of Shakespeare into his life, his case, law, art, theatre, and language -- expect nothing more than what the word in the text can give you; however, you can place in the text, you govern, any word you desire or will. With poetry his play's Act Five gets rid of malice, revenge, death, deaths' heads and caskets and measures motivation or intent in the balance, invoking harmonious, celestial music to drown out Shylock's moans. This is what the romantic, wish-fulfilling, comic main plot attempts to do, in time, and with poetic language succeeds in diminishing the harrowing forces the dramatist has tapped and unleashed.

I believe using Shakespeare's own life experiences the vision becomes more realistic and more complicated than merely a romantic comedy and explains further why Shylock remains on the conscience of an Elizabethan playgoer; because he resonates from Shakespeare's own before bemoaned moan.

The weight and value put upon human wealth as opposed to intrinsic goodness is seen as what distorted Shakespeare's experience and most specifically his father in the area of debts, inheritance and the aggrandizing spirit as it never ends. It converts people into things. Things become more valuable than one's own flesh and blood. Shakespeare's plots in *Merchant of Venice* make everything come out all right, except what is left, in the play, is Shylock; in Shakespeare's life, the author's deprivations and bitter losses. Shakespeare tries to get rid of both but cannot. He can only mitigate their plea. However, instead of death, confiscation of entire estate, treating one's offspring as if they were dead, removal of house, livelihood, the law of mercy, not revenge, provides a remission to a fee, symbolic enough to remember; a gift to their offspring, remaining in house and craft but also a "gift" of *conversion* from miserliness, non-comic response to generosity and the comic response or love. But Shylock does not feel well, nor do we, nor, I believe, did Shakespeare as displacement only works to a point:

PORTIA.
> How far that little candle throws his beams!
> So shines a good deed in a naughty world.
> A substitute shines brightly as a king
> Until a king be by, and then his state
> Empties itself, as doth an inland brook
> Into the main of waters.
>
> (V.i. 90, 91, 94-97)

It is still a naughty world getting and selling late and soon. Perhaps we can isolate that nongenerous spirit and try to convert it; but miserliness and aggrandizement may only be the other side of the same coin as having treasure and being generous.

Shakespeare faces considerable losses in 1596-97 which, I believe I have shown, to have been displaced into the text of his comedy of *Merchant of Venice* and thus artistically handled. It did not get away from him but, as Antonio says at the beginning, that "...makes of me/That I have much ado to know myself." And as Launcelot and Jessica leave one father for better fortune they become "dead" and return as heirs and masters but in that process witness and cannot escape from the dark side and implications of this inheritance. If honest must one be poor like Gobbo? If wealthy, miserly like Shylock? Can the law protect a generous, wealthy, good man like Antonio? Apparently only by, if not the Grace of God, the mercy of Chancery. It did not protect Shakespeare's father. Of this Shakespeare complains both against, and by, his surprise creation, sinning and sinned against, in Shylock. With striking sympathy, and now perhaps a little bit more understood from its contemporary background, Shylock is not totally resolved as the non-accomodatable elements of comedy become the irreducible tragic elements in Shylock's personal tragedy. Capitalism's dark side has been exposed with a sense of sociological realism concentrated in its non-generative, non-comic elements motivated by accumulation, recompense and revenge.

Merchant of Venice with its "pound of flesh" and "quality of mercy" becomes Shakespeare's accurate account of attempting to overcome his own losses by displacement and finally having to painfully attempt to excoriate the unconverted response he cannot psychologically ignore. I believe the melancholy in *Merchant of Venice* and generic problems as a comedy come from Shakespeare's having explored and plummeted his own capacity for, as well as life's limits of, generosity and in the end had to admit he found them both somewhat wanting.

We can differ on matters of interpretation and consequences of making the above disclosures. However we can discern the fact that undeniable, somehow, Shakespeare's life-text impinges upon his dramatic texts at many points. This is true concerning the death of his son and his loss of the case in Queen's Bench on a bond. We can see this at moments in a number of plays from *Comedy of Errors* to *Lear* with Edmund stealing the patrimony as Edmund Lambert, Shakespeare's uncle, did from William. This includes obvious references from the Induction of *Shrew* to Hamlet's legal complaints. Beyond a shadow of a doubt there are autobiographical elements in Shakespeare's plays. Acknowledging this more publicly would go a long way to dispel the popular myths that we know little about Shakespeare or that he did not write the plays. Furthermore, we can begin to put Schoenbaum's excellent work on documents to good use in analyzing the impetus and structure in the plays.

When Shakespeare turned to the text of *Twelfth Night* these matters were on his mind so it was shaped by his life-text as well as being produced to fit the Inns of Court dramatic, legal, festive, and twinning tradition. Many critics of *Twelfth Night* take note of the festive comedy in the play and its passing references to death.[5] No one has acknowledged the relationship between the play and Shakespeare's own twins, let alone that Sebastian, the male twin of Viola, and thought to be dead, is a play-text pattern of the loss of the author's dead twin son as we can discern from the life-text. My analysis of the intertextuality of this phenomenon allows one to further suggest the comic mode or genre selected succeeds by necessity to return the dead twin brother, while reality cannot be that comforting for the playwright. In other words the middle comedies do not just state the case and express anger but seem to give additional text to the life-text, acting out wish-fulfillments, and through their art compensating for real losses. In turn such an analysis of the play-text might help explain why there are so many references to death in a comedy. Then we also see why Shakespeare explores so many myths that may serve to restore one who has been lost; studying Viola/Cesario's emotional response to losing a twin; and represent grief in Olivia's mourning for those who no longer return, but accepting a fictional substitute.

This approach suggests the text coupled with Shakespeare's own biography can shed light on his artistic work as autobiographically charged content, or fictional, or taking form in fictive, attitudes toward his own grief. A grief that might well have reached to stuff out his son's vacant garments with his form and attempt to fill up the room of his absent child.[6] In no way are we trying to psychoanalyze Shakespeare, but we may be able to elucidate Shakespeare's plays by a knowledge of his life and vice versa. We cannot know exactly how he, or any artist, transforms the experiences of his life and the lives he observes around him into the materials of art. Yet we do know, as Virginia Woolf has pointed out, art is woven from such experiences: "...fiction is like a spider's web, attached ever so lightly perhaps, but still attached to life at all four corners. Often the attachment is scarcely perceptible; Shakespeare's plays,...seem to hang there complete by themselves. But when the web is pulled askew,...torn in the middle, one remembers that those webs...are the work of suffering human beings..." Just as readers respond to text, so authors bring to their writings their own crises and losses that then appear in the literary product but are transformed by the literary process. Certainly this is what Virginia Woolf is suggesting. Also, as she says, the literary conventions, or genres, may be stretched by these personal tensions. However this fact of literature has been obliterated by New Criticism and its residual error of the "intentional fallacy". The following does not attempt to explain all of *Twelfth Night*, nor even provide all explanations of the passages cited. It merely attempts to trace resonances, vibrations or crossovers between Shakespeare's life and his play. We will use one event, the fact of his son's death, and note its reverberations in *Twelfth Night*.

Often scholars compare Shakespeare's plays with his sources. By examining how Shakespeare transformed his sources, they have come to insights about themes or issues that were particularly important in the plays themselves. It is my contention that we now can treat Shakespeare's life itself as such a text. That is, we can look at texts from Shakespeare's life, just as we look at written sources to see what themes emerge. As we compare *Twelfth Night* and Shakespeare's life, I find remarkable congruences pointing to the theme of death, the denial of death and the refusal to mourn in *Twelfth Night*. Critics have, like Olivia, continually asked of the play "...what is your text?" "Where lies your text?" (I.v. 237-240.) The answer may be, like Viola's (241), that it is in Shakespeare's bosom as well as his numerous literary sources.

One of these overlappings between the life and the play connects a textual theme to a specific date. The first performance of *Twelfth Night* is recorded as on the day of the anniversary of the baptism of Shakespeare's twin son and daughter. This same record, by a member of that first audience at the Inns of Court, or law schools, caught the foregrounded theme of mourning or loss. As can happen with audiences' response, John Manningham of Middle Temple misplaced the source of the sorrow in the play as evidenced by his referring to Olivia as Malvolio's "lady widdowe", when she is mourning the loss of her brother. Manningham's diary entry following the performance of the play before the Queen in Middle Temple Hall is dated February 2, 1602. This is the very date Shakespeare's own twin daughter Judith and son Hamlet were christened seventeen years earlier in 1585. February 2, 1602 was the seventeenth baptism day of the twins to be celebrated by Judith, but not by Hamlet who had died when he was eleven.

Manningham goes on with rare precision to enumerate some of the other sources for *Twelfth Night* relating to twins. Of these plays he finds it most like *Inganni*, Plautus' *Menaechmi*, and Shakespeare's own earlier twins story, produced also for the Inns of Court at Gray's Inn, *The Comedy of Errors*. Shakespeare has the text of *Twelfth Night* make a connection to this tradition of plays about twins at the law schools before the Queen during the latter portion of Christmas celebrations. Feste refers to "King Gorboduc" and a twinned linguistic pattern "That that is is" (Iv.ii. 17). Between two equal possibilities truth may only be what is successfully asserted as evidenced by this ironic doubling of words. *Gorboduc*, or the *Tragedy of Ferrex and Porrex*, by Sackville and Norton about equal contenders for the throne and a possible source for *Lear*, was presented by the law gentlemen of Inner Temple before Queen Elizabeth at Whitehall, January 18, 1562. Shakespeare's subsequent contribution to this practice was *The Comedy of Errors* on December 28, 1594 before the Queen at Whitehall and later that night at the Inns. In this play he doubles the number of twins from his sources. Although revised for that performance, it has been assumed the play was originally composed in 1588-89, or four years after the birth of his own twins.

Between that production on Holy Innocents Night of 1594 and the composition date of *Twelfth Night*, Shakespeare suffered a tragic loss. Although *Twelfth Night* was first performed in 1602, a reference to the 1599 edition of Hakluyt's *Voyages* and its "new map" (III.iii. 34) could place its composition in 1599. By that date Shakespeare's only son, Hamlet had died in his eleventh year and had been buried August 11,

1596. This was the first immediate death of a family member for Shakespeare, since his father, mother, sister, three brothers, wife and two daughters were still living. *Twelfth Night* celebrates the return of a male twin, thought dead. This central event produces special resonances when set beside the text of Shakespeare's life at the time of the writing of the play and also in 1599. In that year Shakespeare's son would have been thirteen, as his living sister was until just before February 2nd. This age of thirteen years echos through the play in the specific context of death and mourning. Viola announces for purposes of self-identification that her father "...died that day when Viola from her birth/had number'd thirteen years." (V.i. 251-252). The father of the twins in the play had died on their thirteenth birthday. Shakespeare was writing that text in the thirteenth year of his twins' birth when one of them was dead. The recognition scene in the play-text culminates in Sebastian's (V.i. 253-255).

> O, that record is lively in my soul!
> He finished indeed his mortal act
> That day that made my sister thirteen years.

However the twin brother in life had died at eleven. This scene's length and emotional extension may be seen as stretching across Shakespeare's personal wish for return of his lost son more than dramatic expectations would require.

Also, 1599 was Judith's, and would have been Hamlet's, fourteenth birthday. The dramatist has Feste confuse the returned male, supposedly dead, twin with his disguised sister and accepts his generosity: "By my troth, thou has an open hand. These wise men that give fools money get themselves a good report — after fourteen years' purchase." (IV.i. 22-24) However comparable the number is to Shakespeare's life-text it is a glaring legal error, surprising in a play filled with legalisms to be performed before a law school audience. Shakespeare and his father had engaged in such transactions, and he meant to refer to "twelve years," which is the correct term for evaluating land at the price of twelve years' rental. Even though the fool makes the error in number, it is significant that the number chosen could well be the age of the dead son at the time of writing.

Hamlet Shakespeare had been dead three years. In the play Sebastian, thought drowned, has been served by Antonio "for three months" (V.i. 98); and his twin Viola, disguised as a boy, has attended the Duke "three months." As the numbers align between the play and the dramatist's life, so do the moods.

Perhaps it is no accident, then, the play opens with an examination of the mourning process. In the opening scene Valentine reports Olivia is mourning the brother she lost: "...all this to season a brother's dead love, which she would keep fresh and lasting in her sad remembrance." (I.i. 3-32), although Feste chides her for such mourning if he is in heaven (I.v. 63-82). If we return to the text of Shakespeare's life we are reminded Shakespeare had an elder daughter, Susanna, to mourn the loss of her brother Hamlet. Viola mourns her own brother's death in a wholly different fashion, insisting her brother "is in Elysium" (I.ii. 4) but "perchances" he is saved as she herself is (ii. 6-7). In fact, Orsino's first speech, filled with the melancholy of love, sounds more like a displacement for the melancholy of grief, which his sentiments more appropriately describe:

> Give me excess of it, that surfeiting,
> The appetite may sicken, and so die
> That strain again! It had a dying fall:

(I.i. 2-4)

Trying to rid oneself of the feeling of love, at least at Orsino's state of infatuation, is appropriate. This passage seems a more accurate description of one trying to rid himself of grief by a surfeit of mourning.

Other aspects of the play can also be interpreted as similar displacements. The psychological approach of connecting the biographical text to the play's text may suggest the play is serving the author as a vehicle to give form to his own sense of loss. Unlike *Comedy of Errors'* twins, the twins in *Twelfth Night* are, like Shakespeare's own twins, non-identical. In life and the play the death of the male twin has left two sisters in mourning, one of them his twin. Viola, as his twin, can "become" her brother in his absence, becoming what she has lost; and also replaces Olivia's lost brother by becoming a male for her to adore. As we have seen from the dates and ages in the texts, Shakespeare's surviving female twin child is simultaneously a replacement for, or a reminder of, his dead, former eleven-year-old, male twin Hamlet. Thus Viola becomes Cesario:

> Not yet old enough for a man, nor young
> enough for a boy; as a squash is before 'tis
> a peascod, or a codling when 'tis almost an
> apple: 'tis with him in standing water,
> between boy and man. He is very well-favoured
> and he speaks very shrewishly; one would think
> his mother's milk were scarce out of him

(I.v. 166-172)

Shakespeare can find consolation for the loss of an heir in the remaining twin; but the remaining twin cannot find analogous peer consolation until, like Olivia in *Twelfth Night*, she substitutes marriage for her mourning. This does not mean Shakespeare or Viola cease their desire for the male twin's return.

The "perchancing" in the play is an act of imagination or a hope for the return of a lost person. For Viola this is manifested in her hope for Sebastian. For Orsino it is his longing almost to the point of grief for Olivia, whom he will lose. For Olivia it is a mourning for an actually lost brother, displaced in the time-scheme of the play as her present longing upon Cesario, who unknown to her has lost, as Viola, her brother. In the *Twelfth Night* text, then, Shakespeare designs a plot wherein all this perchancing can come true or find its substitution only through the return of Sebastian in the flesh, restoring all losses. The audience is presented with a double vision. They know Sebastian is alive while they enjoy the bitter-sweet study of the characters who mourn and only "fancy" he is alive, or that a brother has been substituted. All this in the face of what mourning teaches: "What's to come is still unsure,/Youth's a stuff will not endure." This is true in fact in the life-text as Susanna, Shakespeare's eldest daughter, will be "sweet and twenty" May 23, 1602, some three months after Middle Temple Hall's first performance of *Twelfth Night* or *What You Will* (cf. II.i. 48-53). Although death is portrayed as inevitable, Sir Toby's comic art insists otherwise as he wishfully sings "But I will never die." (II.iii.114), a definite wish not to be fulfilled except through fictive immortality. The songs sung by other characters who are not in mourning appear to continue this theme of the denial of death and the refusal to mourn. "Come Away Death" ritually removes the trappings of death's identification:

> Not a flower, not a flower sweet,
>   On my black coffin let there be strewn;
> Not a friend, not a friend greet
>   My poor corpse, where my bones shall be thrown:
> A thousand thousand sighs to save
>   Lay me, O where
> Sad true lover never find my grave,
>   To weep there!

$$\text{(II.iv. 60-67)}$$

There is a strong possibility Shakespeare was on tour in the summer in Kent too far in August of '96 to learn of, and return for the burial of his son if the death were unexpected. *Twelfth Night* denies funeral ritual, but the text (oddly enough) for a moment lifts a curtain upon, an extraneous character in the story, the "dead" twin's second sister, who would be congruent with Susanna in Shakespeare's life-texts. Her passion/ mourning is made a twin of Orsino's

> She pined in thought
> And with a green and yellow melancholy
> She sat like patience on a monument,
> Smiling at Grief.

> (II.iv. 115-118)

The curtain falls on this tableau as quickly as it was raised, and if it is meant to be Viola then she has been through Orsino's experience. This is followed by our seeing Viola mourning, in error: "I am all the daughters of my father's house,/And all the brothers too" (ii. 123,124). So graves cannot be found, people will never die, and the dead brother is present; but mourning and its displacement, sorrow and longing, and loss and replacement remain as the twins are yet to be reunited by Shakespeare's art.

It is quite possible then that there are significant emotional crossovers between the *Twelfth Night* text and Shakespeare's life-text. The identification of Hamlet gets displaced upon the remaining twin, the female Judith. This process is paralleled in Viola's disguise as Cesario until Sebastian's return; thus she too "becomes" her twin brother for a time. However, this displacement cannot suffice because it is clearly seen as just a disguise, not a counterfeit; and because it is only a displacement that cannot last. Sebastian, the only son and twin brother must return to replace more permanently Olivia's lost brother. Sebastian enters the vicinity; wanders looking at "memorials" (III.iii. 23). Malvolio appears to be beyond the design of these intended unions because his "love" did not spring from a loss nor was it an outcome of grief. All losses are consoled by the return of Sebastian in the art. This results in some emotional topography and diagraming strikingly similar to Shakespeare's life-text. For instance Hamlet through his own death departs from his twin sister and father, mother and another sister. Sebastian is removed from his twin Viola and father, being removed from him by death, possibly another sister and presumably another. He receives as compensation and replacement Olivia, an anagram for Viola. Viola, like the remaining Judith, loses her twin brother and gets Orsino in marriage, who loved Olivia and lost someone else; ironically to actually happen in Judith's life-text with Thomas Quiney and Margaret Wheeler of Stratford — Oh, Shakespeare's prophetic soul! Olivia (like the elder Susanna) loses her brother and gets the returning twin brother in Sebastian by having overcome her mourning by adoring his "surviving" twin sister. Orsino in a most complex transformation is something like Shakespeare in this family pattern, wanting Olivia (in this case let us see if she is a displacement for his Anne Hathaway, head of Shakespeare's household). He loses her first to the lost male twin and then regains her in a replacement through the twin's "return" and revelation of the object being female rather than male, so finally Anne after grief and displaced love might return her femaleness to the author of the high fantastical grief and melancholy. In the end Orsino has Olivia as a "sister" having gone through parallel loss, longings and returns' and finds direct compensation for the lost male twin son in the female/male disguised Cesario who has miraculously become the female Viola again. It is by no means too much to suggest Shakespeare sees displacement in art, compensation and substitution in life to be the consolation for tragic losses in himself — at least this is what he undeniably provides for each of the major characters. Albeit Malvolio is not so fitted, for his longing does not originate from a loss: perhaps he swaggered more than being aware to shut the gate against thieves. Death will have its revenge but not before this play is done. Wish-fulfillments have been met if the losses were real.

The textual attempt at triumphing over death borrows from the Judeo-Christian tradition. There is, of course, the relevant Christmas sub-theme in which, appropriate to the holiday festival occasion of *Twelfth Night*, the Wise Men bear witness to the Nativity, inadvertently Shakespeare's family double birth date, which after the three-day loss to the world following the Crucifixion will usher in eternal life (no more dying then) through the return of the Son of Man. Sebastian's triumph over death and return from three months' wandering has some smack of divinity in it from both Testaments (Jonah and Christ):

> This youth that you see here
> I snatch'd one half out of the jaws of death,
> Relieved him with such sanctity of love,
> And to his image, which me thought did promise,
> Most venerable worth, did I devotion.

(III.iv. 333-397)

says the Sea Captain, like the Centurion guard at the Crucifixion. Viola, not yet seeing Sebastian in the flesh, sees him in herself, as others saw her: "I my brother know/yet living in my glass;" (III.iv. 413-414). So from loss in both texts to parallel lives. To in the play-text seeing him in the glass and in the life-text seeing the loss of the male twin mirrored in the fiction of *Twelfth Night*. To, in the play-text's wish-fulfillment being realized, a separate male twin being returned. Sebastian removes the need for mourning of the loss and becomes something of a manifested compensation for grief.

Twelfth Night goes on at this rebirth or resurrection to adore the lost object and celebrate the return of its soul. The play, closing the Christmas season, ends with souls returned, dead brothers "redeemed" (V.i. 82), references to sacrificial lambs (133) and reincarnation. The only begotten Son is visited at Twelfth Night by Wise Men who see him who will die and return bringing evidence of the Resurrection. Viola's brother appears with something of the Biblical text mystery: "one face, one voice, one habit, and two persons,/A natural perspective, that is and is not!" (V.i. 223-224). Behind the material, is the spiritual; an illusion, substitute, displacement or replacement is both something and not-the-thing. (Only "that that is is.")

To continue his attempted triumph over death, Shakespeare even draws on Pythagoras and the transmigration of souls for a classical version of such miraculous returns to emphasize his theme:

CLOWN.
What is the opinion of Pythagoras concerning wild fowl?
MALVOLIO.
That the soul of our grandam might happily inhabit a bird.
CLOWN.
What thinkest thou of his opinion?
MALVOLIO.
I think nobly of the soul, and no way approve his opinion.
CLOWN.
Fare thee well. Remain thou still in darkness;
thou shalt hold the opinion of Pythagoras ere I
will allow of thy wits, and fear to kill a woodcock, lest
thou dispose of the soul of thy grandam. Fare thee well.
(IV.ii. 57-64)

Orsino proclaims that a solemn combination shall be made of their dear souls. All losses have been compensated for with the return of the twin.

Shakespeare's concern for twins starts with *Comedy of Errors*, becomes a matter of mourning in *Twelfth Night* and obtains some kind of epitome or resolution in his twin son's namesake play *Hamlet*, as we shall briefly note. Viola will become Orsino's fancy's queen (V.i. 391-397) -- the remaining female twin or the mirroring character in the play -- coming full circle where in his morning-like melancholy he had found "...so full of shapes is fancy/That it alone is high fantastical"

(I.i. 14, 15). Feste enters at the end and cannot keep himself from slipping in a lingering reference to "a little tiny boy" (V.i. 398) from several "texts" and "Our play is done" (I. 416). Behind the comic and sometimes tragic masks of *Twelfth Night* I believe that by looking into the biography we can also discern the author's attempted denials of the face of death. His refusal to succumb to mourning is replaced by the triumphant resurrection or return of the twin brother and only son through his fancy and imaginative art. Finally, in *Hamlet*, wherein Shakespeare played the father's ghost, he is able to put aside the longing for the return of his dead son and allow flights of angels to bear him to an eternal rest.

How has Shakespeare made division of the twin son of his play-text from the one in his life-text? "An Apple cleft in two is not more twin than these two creatures" (V.i. 229-231). Which is Sebastian? For the creative moment, in the mind's eye Shakespeare sees the lost twin son ("A spirit I am indeed") and has him wonder:

> Do I stand there? I never had a brother;
> Nor can there be that deity in my nature
> Of here and everywhere. I had a sister,
> Whom the blind waves and surges have devour'd.
> Of charity, what kin are you to me?
> What countryman? What name? What parentage?
>
> (V.i. 231-238)

What we are witnessing in this notoriously extended recognition scene is not merely Sebastian seeing himself in Viola, for Shakespeare knew from his own that a twin brother and sister can*not* be identical twins, as they are in *The Comedy of Errors*. What we hear also in this text is Shakespeare's own emerging recognition that his imagination has created the substitute in art (the brother Hamlet never had) and that the real twin son has crossed his sea to "The undiscovered country from whose bourn/no traveller returns." Sebastian asks "What parentage?" his other self or his male twin has — answer: both from Shakespeare, but the questioner is, as we now can see, born of Shakespeare's grief of an artful monument like the ones Viola envisions and Sebastian seeks, of Sebastian's life-text "twin", Shakespeare's only but now lost twin son. Hence Judith and Susanna are the only daughters and brothers of their father's house.

Close on the heels of *Twelfth Night* and following a funeral we have *Hamlet*. Shakespeare's brother actor informs us Will played the Ghost in his own play. The dramatist, live father plays the dead father in a play named for his dead son Hamlet. The dead father tells the live son in the play: "Remember me! Remember me!" This is written at the height of "the laws delay" in his case and the dramatist gives Horatio, in his account about Fortinbras, Jr., a legal account in the play-text almost verbatim Shakespeare's case from his life-text:

> HORATIO   ....Who, by a seal'd compact,
> Well ratified by law and heraldry,
> Did forfeit with his life, all those his lands
> Which he stood seized of, to the conqueror:
> Against the which, a moiety competent
> Was gaged by our king; which had return'd
> To the inheritance of Fortinbras,
> Had he been vanquisher; as, by the same covenant,
> And carriage of the article design'd,
> His fell to Hamlet.
> ...to recover of us, by strong hand
> And terms compulsatory, those foresaid lands
> So by his father lost:...
>
> (I.i. 86-95, 102-104 Cf. V.I. 107-126)

Fortinbras by the end of *Hamlet* gains back all his father lost. Clearly this is what Shakespeare is attempting to do in his life.

As Shakespeare is before Chancery, that gate of mercy, that fount of equity, he writes *As You Like It*. This opens with Orlando's complaints against his younger brother, Oliver, who is unjustly keeping his inheritance from him:

> ...obscuring and hiding from me all
> gentlemen-like qualities. The spirit of my
> father grows strong in me, and I will no
> longer endure it: therefore allow me such
> exercise as may become a gentleman,
> or give me the poor allottery my poor
> father left me by testament; with that
> I will go buy my fortunes.
>
> (I.i. 71-77)

The play presents two sons keeping property from their respective brothers -- the elder of each pair, unnaturally, are exiled. The other pair is made up of Duke Senior having been exiled from his rule by Frederick. At the end of the play the second son of Sir Roland tells Duke Senior of Duke Frederick's reformation from his evil ways:

> His crown bequeathing to his banish'd brother,
> And all their lands restored to them again
> That were with him exiled. This to be true,
> I do engage my life.

DUKE SENIOR.
　Welcome, young man;
　Thou offer'st fairly to thy brother's wedding:
　To one his lands withheld and to the other
　A land itself at large, a potent kingdom.

(V.iv. 169-175)

John Shakespeare's estate of Asbies in Wilmcote was being withheld from Shakespeare by his father's brother-in-law's son John. His father had broken the agreement to return upon offering payment of the bond, thus unjustly retaining the dramatist's patrimony. His name was Edmund. Obviously when it comes time for Shakespeare to be thinking about his leaving to, and splitting up of his estates between, his two daughters, his loss to an Edmund will rankle enough to put his namesake into his text and similar chicanery crossing over from the life-text to Edmund's stealing of the patrimony from his half-brother in *King Lear*. By the time of *As You Like It*, Shakespeare has pursued his case as far as the judicial system will permit and, although he does not achieve satisfaction, ultimately the law has recognized his complaints to the utmost. He has not gotten his due, but his due process achieves a stasis. The Bill of Complaint has been completely aired.

Northrup Frye observes about *As You Like It*:

> The appearance of this new society is frequently signalized by some kind of party or festive ritual, which either appears at the end of the play or is assumed to take place immediately afterward. Weddings are most common, and sometimes so many of them occur, as in the quadruple wedding at the end of As You Like It, that they suggest also the wholesale pairing off that takes place in a dance.7

C. L. Barber witnesses in *As You Like It* a balance equally present:

> *As You Like It* seems to me to be the most perfect expression Shakespeare or anyone else achieved of a poise which was possible because a traditional way of living connected different kinds of experience to each other.8

Taming of the Shrew gives vent to anger striking out against the systems; *As You Like It* airs the very objections that produced the anger and reconciles natural feelings with displacement and corruption at a court. In the first Shakespeare satirizes the person causing him pain, in the second he uses art, as he did in *Merchant of Venice*, to address his loss and fictionalize resolutions in his favor as compensatory art. The earnings from his art will be inherited by his daughters. He can use his own language system in drama to pillory a character using another language system from law against him: he can in fiction bring into reality what the other linguistic system will not: "...all...lands restored.../To one his lands withheld...".

So we have seen by these comparisons and re-synchronization of these play-texts with their analogous life-texts Shakespeare's biography does cross over into his drama to produce autobiographical elements. This process has been recognized by other authors, i.e., Virginia Woolf and critics such as David M. Bergeron and Robert Scholes. We have gone on to note not only self-reference but complaint, concern, and preoccupation with personal problems at law and with familial loss. The personal association with twins has the added bonus of linking him to the tradition of twins as subject matter at the Inns of Court and their "festive" and legal associations in *The Comedy of Errors*. The placement into initial positions of his personal self-references, as in *Midsummer Night's Dream*, (first lines) the *Taming of the Shrew*, (Induction), *As You Like It* (first scene) and *Hamlet* (Act I) appear almost as if to instigate or motivate the action, as well as theme, within his generic constraints and shaping mechanisms.[9] The burlesqueness and broad comedy of *Comedy of Errors* and *Taming of the Shrew* appear to be pushed or enervated in coincidence or as synchronicity with his explosive concern for his case and the well-being of his twins who should inherit as he did not. With *Merchant of Venice* and *Twelfth Night* huge swatches of the text seem to be in sympathy with Shakespeare's experience in his court case and his loss of Hamlet his son and heir, a male twin. These plays and *As You Like It* go on to furnish the specifically parallel recompense missing in his life: a triumphant court case, lost land restored, and a male twin, thought dead, returned.

This evidence in the early period of his comedies is obvious with regard to his unfulfilled concern giving way to fictive compensation, if not for him, at least explicitly projected into his characters. They win, as another loses; they are restored after losses; and they are returned after being lost. But for Shakespeare, as well as them: "A substitute shines brightly as a king/Until a king be by, and then his state/Empties itself..." (*Merchant of Venice* V.i. 94-96). Once the solution is seen as only art, a fiction, and recognized as that i.e., "betrays" itself, then the art is not only consoling to the character and compensatory, in some way, for the author, but revealing to both. When the psyche or character can take it and begin to recover, then the process of substitution in reward, return, or compensation is open to scrutiny.

What was the compensation? What was the process? What are the systemic implications? It was dramatic displacement or projection and replacement or symbol substitution through manipulation of language, its structures, its conventions and its building blocks of words, ultimately airy nothing that the dramatic poet has the power to create and recreate. Those words form a web somewhat under the conscious control of the writer, but this is where counter-intentionality emerges and may be evidenced. Within language, drama, and comedy the rules are invoked by mere usage but personal style or impetus pushes up against them at which points they are stretched, broken, or over-ridden and comedy, drama, and language "develops" under the impact of the man that's driving the poet in Shakespeare. It happened to him at law as it happens in law itself for he could and did make it happen on the state: law has its "fictions" as well as its "style." "Nothing is good nor bad only thinking [or rethinking] makes it so." Both may be fashioned in formulation and interpretation.

Forms are to follow, in both the systems of drama and law, so when you wish to assert a "self" in drama or law unpredictable and arbitrary consequences may follow. The results must be manipulated often to continue to preserve the integrity of the system. The astronauts blow up, and, independent of their personal tragedies, they become a part of a "major malfunction" of the system that must be corrected, modified, or abolished. The point is both theatrical and legal systems operate the same way, perhaps all "systems" do: they accept circumstances in conflict, attempt resolutions by compensating or punishing parties upon some norm of human judgement. The result is to modify reality or shift the balance in some way. But essentially the systems allow the judge or dramatist to have his way by certain rigorously prescribed procedures. In the process the winner is "right," the loser "wrong" and the system upheld by judicious utterances. This procedure can be scrutinized and played with at law: "...it appertaineth to our princely care and office only to judge over all our Judges and to discern and determine such differences as at any time may or shall arise before our several Courts, touching the jurisdiction and the same to settle and decide..." (Bacon for King James).[10] Chancery does this with equity rulings by appearing to be merciful upon exceptions or overruling lower courts and mitigating the plea against the written law and thus achieving obvious fairness in the particular case. "We...do will and command, that our Chancellor... shall not hereafter desist unto our subjects upon their several complains...such relief in equity (not withstanding any former proceedings at common law against them) as shall stand with true merits and justice of their cases..." (Bacon for King James).

Likewise, in Shakespeare's later comedies and particularly in *Measure for Measure*, comedy, character and action, as they are played with, reveal (or *betray*) how the conventions are arbitrarily manipulated to have things happen as a King, a Duke, a character, an author or an audience might wish. It is of interest, then, that the play was first designed for a private performance before King James at Hampton Court. It is at this conjunction, as we shall see more explicitly in the next chapter, that Shakespeare's counter-intentionality,[11] linguistic betrayal and legal fictions are explicitly revealed. *Measure for Measure*, in achieving balance, exposing inappropriate measures and law, and attempting absolute justice may disclose the law's tyrannical presuppositions. In other words, in Shakespeare's career and King James' concern for the law, both of them play with these systems of language in similar ways (dramatist as judge and Judge as Dramaturge) betraying the fiction to the users as they realize their power to manipulate their recipients. With systems stripped bare of their rigging and the Captains exposed to their elements, the manipulators are in sympathy with their very nature -- making them victims and victors at once as Prospero so eloquently describes:

> In few, they hurried us aboard a bark,
> Bore us some leagues to sea; where they prepared
> A rotten carcass of a boat, not rigg'd
> Nor tackle, sail, nor mast; the very rats
> Instinctively have quit it: there they hoist us,
> To cry to the sea that roar'd to us, to sigh
> To the winds whose pity, sighing back again,
> Did us but loving wrong.
>
> (*The Tempest*. I.ii. 144-151)

Shakespeare's awareness of justice, dependent upon law, and law itself based upon fictive techniques and skill in a person achieves the perception level of The Tempest, about nature, life, drama, language and law; in which sympathetic utterances could do "loving wrong" to the plaintiff -- counter-intentionally.

The systems reveal themselves; a victim is overwhelmed by them and a victor rules them. In Measure for Measure the Duke recognizes in Old Escalus that:

> The nature of our people,
> Our city's institutions, and the terms
> For common justice, you're as pregnant in

As art and practice hath enriched any
That we remember.

(I.i. 10-14).

As for Angelo "Mortality and mercy in Vienna/Live in thy tongue and heart: (ii. 45-46). Shakespeare knows the power of language, its counter-intentionality, to fulfill and betray itself, reveal its intent and expose its opposite. He dramatizes this in *Measure for Measure* using the system of law language as well to do it: to be lawful you have to be illegal; to be just you have to be unfair; to be merciful you must be cruel; and to be pure you must kill, all presided over by a substitute puritanical Duke who is corrupt and a real Duke whose compassion exposes his tyranny. Just as Shakespeare reveals this counter-intentionality in the law and the dramatic language of his own play it is being discussed and handled in the law-text language itself:

> ...forasmuch as mercy and justice be the true supports of our Royal Throne...our subjects...should not be abandoned, and exposed to perish under the rigour and extremity of our laws:...
>
> (Bacon for King James)

Our law will correct the law when its "counter-intentionality" becomes evident. The language of our law will be modified to grant what is desired for justice, despite what the law or a judge or a court says. Bacon, who had been present at *Gesta Grayorum*, is saying for the King at law what Shakespeare is dramatizing before the same King in *Measure for Measure*: the language systems can produce what you will when we fully understand they do operate in response to our tongue that utters the desires of our heart. Careful, you may get what you really want, not what you ought to have. You may want power or position but you may be controlled by it and not be able to do what you wanted to do.

Chapter IV

Before King James: Betrayal and Revelation[1]

DUKE.
> Thyself and thy belongings
> Are not thine own so proper as to waste
> Thyself upon thy virtues, they on thee.
> Heaven doth with us as we with torches do,
> Not light them for themselves; for if our virtues
> Did not go forth of us, 'twere all alike
> As if we had them not. Spirits are not finely touch'd
> But to fine issues, nor Nature never lends
> The smallest scruple of her excellence
> But, like a thrifty goddess, she determines
> Herself the glory of a creditor,
> Both thanks and use. But I do bend my speech
> To one that can my part in him advertise;
> Hold therefore, Angelo: -
> In our remove be thou at full ourself;
> Mortality and mercy in Vienna
> Live in thy tongue and heart: old Escalus,
> Though first in question, is thy secondary.
> Take thy commission.

ANGELO.
> Now my good lord,
> Let there be some more test made of my mettle,
> Before so noble and so great a figure
> Be stamp'd upon it.

Measure for Measure I.i. 30-51

We have seen in early plays where the references are personal, the texts being presented in the Inns of Court and the court cases represented in the play-texts fulfilling or compensating for the legal-texts. Now we will see Shakespeare use legal-texts before the King himself and his high-level juristic audience. The dramatist will turn those texts into dramatic fiction to show the lawyers they are no freer from the linguistic and fictive tricks, play and manipulation than the players. In his dramatic text Shakespeare can restore lands or return a twin. Just as Timon with but a word can give away his lands, so Angelo with but a word can condemn a man to death. Isabella remarks upon these paltry assumptions:

> ...man, proud man,
> Drest in a little brief authority,
> Most ignorant of what he's most assured,
> His glassy essence, like an angry ape,

> Plays such fantastic tricks before high heaven
> As make the angels weep;...

Measure for Measure (II.ii. 117-123)

The limits of authority are revealed to expose the arbitrariness behind the controls of the theatrical and legal language systems. In *Measure for Measure*, performed before the new King in 1603, Shakespeare seems to stand, like his Duke, outside the action, watching the plots demonstrate how the language of drama can manipulate the language of law to bring about desired and arbitrary ends for the sake of balance, or measure for equal measure. He and the energy, or motivating force, seem to be beyond anger, mere stasis, balance, or compensation. He is in a position to look upon both crafts and witness the manipulative power of language as well as its ability to be manipulated by power. Recognition follows that both language systems can betray, let down and reveal, the user: the language of law will betray one party to the justice of the other, and the language of drama will betray the audience into believing real, rather than only fictional, justice has been served. Realizing this is to find oneself outside both systems looking in, glimpsing, appreciating, the complexity, contradictoriness, ambiguity and ultimate manipulations of both language systems.

In *Anatomy of Criticism* (p. 174) Northrup Frye sees the Duke in *Measure for Measure* as the "*architectus*" carrying out the desire of the author to reach a happy ending; an older man begins the action of the play by withdrawing from it, ending the play by returning and gaining his freedom as a reward of his exertions. C. L. Barber (*Shakespeare's Festive Comedy*, p. 249) suggests *Measure for Measure* is a courtesy book, one that instructs, teaching object lessons. The whole of *Measure for Measure* is like a political, moral and legal instruction manual dramatized with a hierarchy of proper behavioral models as it attempts to correct a society gone wrong at all levels. This course culminates in Isabella, a Jacobean Portia-Mercy figure, instructing the Duke in the particular nature of English law after its arbitrariness has earlier been revealed in Angelo's enforcing or qualifying "...the laws/As to [his] soul seems good." (I.i. 66-67) and "...Mortality and mercy in Vienna/Live in [his] tongue and heart..." (ii. 45-46). Law's subtlety rests on highly ambiguous and arbitrary assertions, as revealed by the state of Angelo's soul: "Ignomy in ransom and free pardon/Are of two houses: lawful mercy/Is nothing kin to foul redemption." (II.iv. 111-113). How is that to be determined but by the intent of the judge, and that without "counter-intentionality"? How is intent on the part of the defendant to be determined except by representing it in court through some oratorical and rhetorical skill, akin to creating characters on the stage through a literary text. Both engage in the same linguistic techniques of *imitatio*. Subjects' intents only become actionable by English law if they are in fact enacted. If merely thought or just uttered without consequent result or action, constituting evidence of a conspiracy, "...you but waste your words". However, a judge can breathe mercy between his lips and an act of execution will be withheld, although required by law. A dramatist's words are wasted unless they are enacted. As about a defendant, Isabella says:

> His act did not o'ertake his bad intent,
> And must be buried as but an intent
> That perished by the way. Thoughts are no subjects,
> Intents but merely thoughts.

> (V.i. 455-460)

Shakespeare's father intended to pay his loan but the resulting action did not prove that before the law. The above "decision" in *Measure for Measure* is nearly that from *Hales v. Pettit*, a case in *Plowden's Reports*, that Shakespeare had already cited in the grave-diggers scene in *Hamlet* about Ophelia's suicide:

> For the imagination of the mind to do wrong
> without an act done, is not punishable in our law;
> neither is a resolution to do that wrong,
> which he does not, punishable, but the
> doing of the act is the only point which the
> law regards...

Intents are no more than performative utterances. For Shakespeare this applies to himself, his characters, as well as his father, and to the Justices and King now present in his audience.

In *Measure for Measure*, Shakespeare goes beyond personal vendetta to look critically at the language system of law at a time when it was doing so itself. He sees it to be like drama in which the outcome is determined not by law but by utterances determined by the judge that likewise contain their own counter-intentionality. If so, then a mercy figure controlled by the dramatist can utter superior law by the same arbitrary intent through the conventions of a language system that comes into a law-text from the King, Bacon, Chancellor Ellesmere, or Justice Coke of King's Bench. These theatrical conventions allow the dramatist to carry out his wish. As most current analyses of *Measure for Measure* agree, the Duke in the last scene confuses theatricality and life-like theatre by manipulating characters. Shakespeare reveals in this counter-intentionality that the arbitrary determination of law and drama on life itself is equally indistinguishable, or undifferentiable, and equally fictive in the face of real-life human emotions. That providing measure for equal measure in law, drama or life necessitates at best a Procrustean bed appears to be the message of this play.

Measure for Measure reveals the latter phases of Shakespeare's attitudinal development toward his encounters with the legal system we have been tracing. Shakespeare was angry at a defendant in *Taming of the Shrew* and used fiction to vent that anger. Shakespeare expressed fictional restoration in *Merchant of Venice* and *As You Like It* to compensate for injustice dealt him by the legal system. In *Measure for Measure* Shakespeare realizes, looking from outside the judicial and dramatic language systems, that to provide measure for measure in these linguistic systems requires an understanding that they are arbitrary, ambiguous, and manipulated by words. Intent itself can only be enacted through a controllable language system. However, law stands, and drama works through changes in language and convention. This can only have been corroborated by looking at other texts for intertextuality, as does Frye, and outside the text for contextuality in other texts suggested by Barber. This method is sustained in our case by law (legal language system) and autobiography (Shakespeare's personal life-text). Contextualizing these plays as foregrounds, from Shakespeare's court case in the background, substantiates the feeling that *Taming of the Shrew* comes from subjective agitation unresolved; *As You Like It* from balanced resolution; and *Measure for Measure* from objective anatomization of a fictive language system we agree to use to give order to our arbitrary lives.

This evidence suggests Shakespearean comedy proceeds from an arena within which autobiographical issues may be aired; through a period of wish-fulfilled resolutions; beyond the very process of such complex resolutions, where it may be manipulated and studied. Thus *Comedy of Errors* may be seen as an opportunity to air the unique problems confronted by Shakespeare as father of twins; *Twelfth Night* (and *Hamlet*) may represent his attempts at resolving the death of his twin son; and *Winter's Tale* and *Tempest* explore the manipulation of time and space to bring about family happiness that the author so desperately and irrevocably desired.

Measure for Measure comes at the moment when Shakespeare was reconciled to loss of a son in *Hamlet* and *Twelfth Night*, the losses in inheritance in *As You Like It*, and his court case in *Merchant*. He is promoted into the King's Men where he can view power, control, and government up close and even play to it directly. Not surprising, then, that perhaps some coherence can be found in the text of *Measure for Measure* as a type of treatise-like law-text, dramatized for King James VI of Scotland as a lesson in English law, courts, and procedure as he became James I of England.

After 1603 and the death of Queen Elizabeth, the new English King James, with his principles of Divine Right, becomes the throned Monarch. Insofar as Scotland had no separate jurisdiction for equity as England did, Chancery was threatened from a new direction by the King's desire to assert his prerogative. Particularly ominous was his ordering a pickpocket hanged without trial during his Progress from Scotland to London.[2] Because of plague, this Progress ended with the King residing at Hampton Court outside London, where Shakespeare's *Measure for Measure*, performed in 1604, was designed for his entertainment. The play served as a complicated reflection, almost a mirror, for Shakespeare and His Majesty. Shakespeare analyzes the legal system he had experienced after disappointment, but from a position of theatrical power, and the play-text mirrors legal issues facing King James. It raises the issues about using the law to interfere arbitrarily with the fabric of society by either too strict or too loose a following of the law and its letter—what is known as equity of statute, allowing interpretation on the part of the magistrate.[3]

Angelo, the Duke of Vienna's deputy or replacement, allowing the real Duke to be an experimental observer, is attempting a moral reformation of Viennese society by rigorous interpretation of statutes, exposing their flaws and counter-intentionality, as in condemning legitimate sex in the name of righteousness. It can be quite impractical, counterproductive, and immoral to alter custom by a rigid application of the law. The returning Duke, on the other hand, engages in rectifying Angelo's administrative difficulties. This betrays the system and exposes the disruption or unpredictability caused by personal and arbitrary manipulation of the judicial apparatus, even if it is for the purpose of offering remedy for injustices. The intervention by prerogative action, be it by Duke, King, dramatist or writer, despite commendable motive or intent, nevertheless clearly does violence to precedent, form, due process and procedure designed to protect the law and preserve individual rights, character, unity of the art, and boundaries of genre. King James was being exposed to flaws and weaknesses in his judges, instructed in how to be humane and just, and how to follow English precedent. The professional audacity of Shakespeare's play-text is tempered by the convention of art educating in the tradition of an

Inns of Court entertainment, such as *Gorboduc* performed before the
Queen, or in *Mirror for Magistrates*.

In *Measure for Measure*, Shakespeare has Vincentio, the Duke of
Vienna, give Angelo the very power of equity reserved for King James:
"...your scope is as mine own,/So to enforce or qualify the laws/As to
your soul seems good." (I.i. 65-67). King James allowed his Chancellor
to be the Keeper of the Seal, the power Elizabeth was reluctant to
delegate to Ellesmere when he was hers.

> Hold therefore, Angelo. —
> In our remove be thou at full ourself;
> Mortality and mercy in Vienna
> Live in thy tongue and heart: old Escalus,
> Though first in question, is thy secondary.
> Take thy commission.
>
> (I.i. 43-48)

Angelo, mirroring the Court of King's Bench, represents strict
application of the law and, like Portia as equity and Chancery,
Isabella is the mercy-figure, parodied by the bawd "Madam Mitiga-
tion" (I.ii. 45):

> ISABELLA.
> No ceremony that to great ones 'longs,
> Not the king's crown nor the deputed sword,
> The marshal's truncheon nor the judge's robe,
> Become them with one half so good a grace
> As mercy does.
>
> (II.ii. 77-81)

This had repeated appeal for James, as did Portia's mercy speech, in
which the quality becomes the monarch better than his crown, for he
asked to see in this very season *The Merchant of Venice* a second time in
the same week. Isabella is even more conceptually specific about these
subtle technical differences in equity between pity and clemency when
it pertains to judicial discretion:

> Ignomy in ransom and free pardon
> Are of two houses: lawful mercy
> Is nothing kin to foul redemption.
>
> (II.iv. 111-113)

Here is another example of "counter-intentionality" with regard to
reward, restitution, compensation or the opposite of the desired
punishment in order to lead man to justice. In the attempt to forgive but

not forget, mercy, or suspended or reduced sentences, may result in rewarding crime or condoning it.

Shakespeare's play-text joins the law-texts of the period. Shakespeare's Jacobean mercy-figure Isabella has learned from the equity writers, such as William Lambarde and Edward Hake, a concern for case law and precedent, which prevent misuse of prerogative powers (see Endnote 3). Isabella appeals to these texts in her drama-text. She does so against a double threat. First she confronts a tyrannically strict constructionism, that of Angelo's "...It is the law, not I...", threatening the area of interpretation or equity of statute. Secondly, she must deal with an equally tyrannical personal intervention in the law, that of the Duke, who attempts to punish and reward those whom he favors. William West of Inner Temple, where *Twelfth Night* was performed, wrote *Symboleography* in 1594, which provided an analogous if not a legal source-text for *Comedy of Errors*. Thomas Ashe of Gray's Inn, where *Comedy of Errors* was performed, wrote *Epieikeia*, or a Treatise on Equity, published in 1608, four years after *Measure for Measure*. However, both write in their law-texts, establishing the legal framework of Shakespeare's comedies, that equity is called "equal" and a "reasonable measure." This helps interpret the legal technicality, as well as the Biblical significance, of this very play's title. These references underscore the state-of-the-art philosophical, theological, legal, political, and social issues the problematical justice Shakespeare is presenting in *Measure for Measure*'s play-text. Shakespeare's life-text court case enters his plays but by *Measure for Measure* the text is penetrated from the legal-texts and issues raised by King James, Bacon, Yelverton, Plowden, Lambarde, Ellesmere, Coke, St. Germain, West and Hake. These will be picked up by the Puritans and Perkins as they concern themselves with current arguments concerning equity, mercy, interpretation, intent, redemption, pardon, and prerogative judicial powers in conflict with the strictness of English common law.

These seemingly metaphysical problems, as in life, so in the play, are based upon or find their arguments over a secular legal case. Isabella, the plaintiff, pleads for the release of her brother, unjustly adjudged a criminal, who has received the death penalty as an example of strict justice. He has been charged with fornication for getting his betrothed with child, what Shakespeare committed when impregnating Anne Hathaway with his firstborn, Susanna. Angelo, the Deputy for the absent Duke, is willing to release his prisoner if Isabella, who is about to become a nun, will sleep with him. As in *Twelfth Night* a sister here is also attempting to restore a brother thought to have been lost, reminiscent of the life-text of Shakespeare's daughter Judith losing her brother-twin Hamlet. Angelo, not getting his way, hides behind a strict judicial interpretation:

ANGELO.
    Your brother is a forfeit of the law,
    And you but waste your words.
ISABELLA.
    Why all the souls that were were forfeit once,
    And he that might the vantage best have took
    Found out the remedy. How would you be
    If he which is the top of judgment should
    But judge you as you are? O, think on that!
    And mercy then will breathe within your lips
    Like man new made.
ANGELO.
    Be you content fair maid,
    It is the law, not I, condemn your brother.

(II.ii. 70-80)

Here dramatic-text presents a particularly thorny problem in common law when equity is not being applied and law has unjust results. William West's law-text provides a description of what Angelo is doing in the play-text, when he writes in *Symboleography* (A₂):

> Other lawyers do term it *Summum Jus*, Law in the highest degree or most exact, and it is so taken of them when man stands more upon the letter of the Law. In which behalf, it so falleth out oft times, that under a colour of knowledge of the Laws, many grosse and dangerous errors be committed.

The very danger of absolute law is in its exposing counter-intentionality if the letter is so adhered to as to produce injustice.

Angelo, the strict constructionist, absolute legist, and practitioner of *Summum Jus*, is removed at his return by the lenient Duke. However, what effect does this have on justice administered from identical laws? The human element of judicial replacement is to be dramatized. Angelo is brought to trial; the judges are judged by prerogative rule. But this raises the issue bothering Edward Hake at this time, that of the "...constitutional right of injunctions against enforcing a right and imprisoning one who has followed form of law" (p. v). Technically the Duke is seeking to investigate, try, and convict Angelo for carrying out the laws he was deputized to enforce.

In this new case, which concerns the same issue, now includes Angelo's sleeping with his own betrothed, as it turns out, the intent then would be on trial, as it was not allowed to be in Claudio's case. Representing Chancery's use of equity, Isabella changes from one who has just argued against the severity of the law and for mercy in her brother's case. In this capacity she insists upon the equity of following the common law to achieve mercy by observing English law's regard for pure intent as non-actionable. Using a different form of equity to achieve the merciful end; equity of statute or ruled interpretation v. equity of judicial discretion or free pardon. England's laws recognize treasonable acts but not conspiracy in the American sense: conspiracy is not a criminal act.

> For Angelo,
> His act did not o'ertake his bad intent,
> And must be buried as but an intent
> And perished by the way. Thoughts are no subjects,
> Intents but merely thoughts.
>
> (V.i. 455-460)

King James and Coke take notice! This reflects Isabella's subsequent role of dispensing forgiveness, clemency, and mercy, but it is also precisely the equity decision handed down by Queen's Council in *Hales v. Pettit.* Shakespeare had already used portions of the case, wherein it was decided that the water did not come to the victim, Ophelia, found in Plowden's *Commentaries* on Reports of 1550 to 1580 in *Hamlet.* The decision, in part, reads:

> For the imagination of the mind to do wrong without an act done, is not punishable in our law; neither is a resolution to do that wrong, which he does not, punishable, but the doing of the act is the only point which the law regards...

Benefitting a bad intent, but to the detriment of only an offer to pay a debt, English common law and Chancery do not recognize intent without evidence of an overt act.

So Shakespeare, in plays like *Merchant* and *Measure,* and apparently to the King's delight, dramatizes law-texts before the Court by analyzing and putting forth for scrutiny English v. Scottish jurisprudence, precedent, and case law. Through Isabella, Shakespeare's text as before, presents the necessity of Chancery, absent in Scottish law, for remedy, but not to replace, common law in King's Bench. At the same time in both *Merchant*'s letter-of-the-law interpretation (not a drop of blood in the pound of flesh) and *Measure*'s following a Queen's (King's) Council case, Shakespeare shows Chancery (Portia and Isabella) directing the procedure of the respective Dukes. This makes clear the prerogative avenues of mercy before King James in Chancery. These do not merely act as an arm of arbitrary, prerogative authority because they must follow the intent of statute and abide by their own case precedents as in *stare decisis*. Equity follows the law, thereby fulfilling it.

There is no question but that early in his reign the King heard Shakespeare's play-text interpenetrated by law-texts, and the playwright's dramatization of subtle contradictions pertaining to equity. From the account of Edmund Tylney, Master of the Revels, for the year from November 1, 1604 to October 31, 1605, one finds the following seven plays that reveal law-textual matters inserted by Shakespeare performed before King James. It is almost as if with the death of Lambarde Shakespeare participated on behalf of a strong Chancery, or at least its use by King James, advocated by Ellesmere, Lambarde's texts, and the rise of Bacon against Coke.

> November 1, 1604 - "The Mour of Venis" (*Othello*), the first recorded performance.
>
> The Sunday following - The *Merry Wives of Windsor*.
>
> December 26, 1604 (St. Stephen's Night) - *Measure for Measure*, the first recorded performance.
>
> December 28, 1604 (Innocents' Night) - "The plaie of Errors" (*The Comedy of Errors*).
>
> Between New Year's Day and Twelfth Night (January 6, 1605) - *Love's Labour's Lost*.
>
> January 7, 1605 - "the play of Henry the Fifth" (*Henry V*).
>
> Shrove Sunday, 1605 - *The Merchant of Venice*.
>
> Shrove Tuesday - a play called the *Merchant of Venice*, again Commanded by the King's Majesty.

It is of interest to note connections between Shakespeare's life and the writing of his plays and, as we saw in *Twelfth Night*, the performance date and his life. The performance dates in the case of *Comedy of Errors* we have seen as important. But particularly interesting in the Jacobean period is not when they were written only, but when they were performed in His Majesty's presence.

From November 1604 until Shrove Tuesday 1605, the Christmas season, Tylney was serving up from Shakespeare a menu of his observations on the particular brands of English justice and law, equity and mercy, with their courts and jurisdictions. *Othello* presents the trial of Othello in the Council-Chamber of Venice (I.ii.), where law-text arguments for state necessity override Brabantio's personal claims on his daughter. The very beginning of *The Merry Wives of Windsor* offers references to contempt of court and Star Chamber, followed by later personal references to the Inns of Court. *Measure for Measure*, as we have seen, has Isabella go through her various trials, hearings, and prison scenes, as well as explicitly engaging in high-level discourse on matters of common law, mercy, and equity. *The Comedy of Errors* contains Shakespeare's first use of legal-texts pertaining to equity in Aegeon's trial and the Duke's clemency. *Love's Labour's Lost* contains various penalties, decrees, explicit use, and intertextuality from William West's treatise on equity, *Symboleography*'s "what manner and form following..."), duties of a Chancery solicitor (cf. II.i.), and "quillets." In Act II, scene ii, *Henry V* dramatizes the trial and discourse on appeals and the King's mercy. Capping all these command performances is the prototype of the representation of equity and mercy in Portia of the *Merchant of Venice*. Evidence that this exemplary menu in some way pleased the King, interested him or at least did not offend, exists in his requesting a repeat performance of *The Merchant of Venice* (clearly the most legally oriented of these plays) within three days of the first performance in private audience at Court.

In the same season in private performances with royal approval, the King witnessed law-text in the play-texts of Shakespeare. These dramatized seven specific practical demonstrations of the theoretical principles of English equity. He observed the recognition in Council of national necessity over family claims (two conflicting rights adjudicated at highest level for the greatest benefit) in *Othello*. He heard about the power of equity to quickly handle riots endangering national security in Star Chamber in *Merry Wives of Windsor* (I.i.). He was audience to equity decisions following precedent of the King's Bench (top of common law) in *Measure for Measure*. Equity is exercised by the head of state, according to a balance between statute law and natural law (equity of statute) in *Comedy of Errors*. James witnessed equity, or reason, allowing human necessity (love) to prevail over arbitrary decree in *Love's Labour's Lost*. Shakespeare dramatized for him the King's mercy or equity as recognized but not exercised to the detriment of the realm in *Henry V*. Finally, he twice saw equity achieved by a most rigorous adherence to the written letter of the law (*lex scripta* -- exclusively a pound of flesh) in *Merchant of Venice*. Equity in these cases in the plays ranged from strict adherence, through expedience and overriding circumstances to possibility of suspended sentence in court systems ranging from King's Council, Star Chamber, Chancery, King's Bench, Exchequer and Admiralty (where mercantile and natural law are tinged by Roman law), which covers all of the English Royal prerogative jurisdictions. The author of these texts had just been through three years of legal struggle in Chancery, as many in Queen's Bench and earlier courts of common law at lower levels.

These life-texts and law-texts were produced for James in play-texts at the time the King was seriously considering modifications in these exclusively English judicial institutions. He contemplated amalgamating them and bringing them under his direct control, a modification that did not take place in British history until after the impact of *Bleak House*. The King most likely paid attention once or twice in one week to a passage, perhaps modified from the original reference to the Queen, about mercy or equity:

> 'Tis mightiest in the mightiest, it becomes
> The throned monarch better than His crown;...
> > *Merchant of Venice* (IV.i. 188-189)

Josephine Waters Bennett in her "*Measure for Measure*" *as Royal Entertainment*[4] suggests the Duke was designed by Shakespeare to imitate King James, not only to merely flatter but to offer him an objective study of himself. This presumes a considerable familiarity with the Monarch and presumption on Shakespeare's part. However, I believe, that she has caught the serious issues in the content of the play and the objective or analytical mode in which they are presented. The play itself was probably conceived in the humanistic concept of court entertainment, as were those at the Inns of Court, for festive entertainment but also, if not didactic, at least worthy of the intellectual inquiry characteristic of the scholarly new monarch. The other plays, clearly not originally written for that purpose, seem by this conjunction to have been selected and produced to amplify by proximity these intellectualized legal concerns about equity and the Royal jurisdictions Shakespeare could look back upon with objectivity from his own personal experiences. Above all, these plays presented speeches before judges, Chancellors, and monarchs, in the text and in the audience at the same time, about their responsibility to law and justice in exercising their power of equity and mercy.

These preoccupations in Shakespeare's mind are mirrored in King James' historical confrontation with these principles. This appears most clearly in Sir Francis Bacon's and Henry Yelverton's summation of a Commission's findings in the case of *Glanvill v. Courtney*, wherein the Crown sides with Chancery over and against the common law in King's Bench on July 18, 1616.

Now, forasmuch as mercy and justice be the true supports of our Royal Throne, and that it properly belongeth to us, in our princely office, to take care and provide, that our subjects have equal and indifferent justice ministered to them; and that where their case deserveth to be relieved in course of equity, by suit in our Court of Chancery, they should not be abandoned, and exposed to perish under the rigour and extremity of our laws: — We...do will and command, that our Chancellor, or Keeper of the great Seal, for the time being, shall not hereafter desist unto our subjects upon their several complains (now or hereafter to be made) such relief in equity (not withstanding any former proceedings at common law against them) as shall stand with true merits and justice of their cases, and with the former ancient and continued practice and proceeding of our Chancery; and that it appertaineth to our princely care and office only to judge over all our Judges, and to discern and determine such differences as at any time may or shall arise before our several Courts, touching the jurisdiction and the same to settle and decide as we in our princely wisdom shall find to stand most with our honour, and the example of our Royal Progenitors, in the best time, and the general weal and good of our people, for which we are to answer unto God, who hath placed us over them:...5

In short, despite the Divine Right of Kings principle, James would allow Chancery in his name to correct through equity the errors and injustices in common law in lower courts, as we and he had seen dramatized on several occasions in Portia and Isabella and many of Shakespeare's plays. Even if they didn't influence him, they certainly reinforced, or were not antagonistic to, his views. They in turn were not influenced by his views initially because his propensity was otherwise. He continued seeing a greater number of performances of these plays during Shakespeare's lifetime. In fact as James saw more, Shakespeare wrote less, and became more involved in producing the plays he had written on those themes.6 He might write one or two a year but he was involved in producing seven to ten as they were edited, augmented, and had to not contain material getting the playwright in trouble (cf. Kernan, pp. 60, 63, 79, 182-83, 204). The whole area of Shakespeare's production and writing in connection with James's thought and issues and their interrelationship is fascinating: One remembers that King James' sons to inherit were born the Dukes of Albany and Cornwell (titles Lear's bad daughters marry into) and James' Queen was from Elsinore in Denmark. There is no question that to some degree Shakespeare's life-text experience of remaining close to the throne, and dramatization before it, formed a loop between his life-text, law-text, play-text and Royal life/law texts.7

The above support for Chancery and its Courts of Equity influenced by Ecclesiastical law and practices was signed for King James by Sir Francis Bacon (*Per Ipsum Regum* [sic] Francis Bacon). Bacon clearly knew in the above quotation that what reached Bacon's and

Ellesmere's ears from law-texts and Shakespeare's play-texts, and earlier at the Inns of Court before the Queen in *Comedy of Errors*, would be welcomed by the ear of the very monarch who had repeated to him, from Shakespeare's *Merchant of Venice*; "And earthly power doth then show likest God's/When mercy seasons justice."

The harmony of Shakespeare's play-text and this law-text attests to the dramatist's life-text synchronicity with the developments at Court in these complex, theoretical, and comical matters of State. What needs particular attention in the specifically delicate blend of *Measure for Measure* is the fact Bacon's Commission insists on all judges being subject to the top of judgment, in this case not Angelo and the Duke advised by Isabella, but King James being advised by the Chancellor through Chancery (see Bacon's Commission above). In addition, James is to be accompanied by, or act through the Gate of Mercy, having all superior justice in any case meted out according to former practice and precedents resident in Chancery. These are principles we have seen represented in the plays by Isabella and Portia. This is certainly reflected in the legal instruction Shakespeare had incorporated into *Measure for Measure*, wherein the Duke oversees and overrides Angelo, thereby judging his judges, but with the advice of Isabella, the mercy-figure signifying the advice and opinion of the Chancellor according to the equitable procedures of Chancery.

Shakespeare can no longer be seen as merely a passive recipient quoting law-text or just imitating his times. He is providing opinion and siding with certain judicial opinions. In at least the one area of equity, he vigorously advocates English jurisprudence, with its unique existence of Chancery, alongside King's or Queen's Bench. He entered the arena of these debates and developments in a number of ways. He introduced law-texts into his play-texts performed before members of the Inns of Court and judicial audience members, emphasizing the humane and equitable applications of the law overriding the letter of the law in statutes and decrees presented in *Comedy of Errors*, *Love's Labour's Lost* and *A Midsummer Night's Dream*. His own case of *Shakespeare v. Lambert*, so hotly pursued in Chancery, certainly encouraged the kind of cases reaching the Mastership level of Chancery. These finally brought about equity of redemption for bonds and grace periods in mortgages and loans, evidenced by the writings concerning these matters by the Masters of Chancery, William Lambarde and George Carew. Initially only in connection with his case but then in production before the King twice, the play-text became almost a law-text in the struggle between Chancery (Chancellor Ellesmere and Bacon) against Sir Edward Coke and common law, dramatizing the necessity of recognizing the equity of statute as a right of Chancery to give protection to subjects, interpreting as the King's conscience his absolute law (*summum jus*). This also permits the King to retain that prerogative source of law over common law, and Chancery its role of reconciling the King to the common law. As Ellesmere said "You'll [King James] be but the Duke of Venice", not having benefit of instructions or interpretation making one's utterances more acceptable by the lower courts.

Shakespeare's two performances of *The Merchant of Venice* before the King clearly anticipate Bacon's Commission for the King, which declared upon *Glanvill v. Courtney* that equity (Chancery) must be maintained in its supremacy over the common law to protect the citizen against the rigorous, and sometimes unjust strict application, or misapplication, of the law, hence offering mercy as well as justice. His production of *Measure for Measure*, and later *The Winter's Tale*, was designed to present for the new King's contemplation the legal problems arising from the consequences of interference by tyrannical use of English law.

Unquestionably Shakespeare's life-text and play-texts impinge upon legal history for performances before his use of law-texts with juristic audiences. Shakespeare enters this discourse at a point where its influence carries over into the American system of appellate courts, which was shortly to be constructed by lawyers who had been members of the Inns. Contextuality and intertextuality suggest that in this area of equity, involving for Shakespeare a long, deliberate and energetic personal pursuit, his artistic creations are definitely in the context of legal history that anticipated and participated in the changes in English laws pertaining to equity.

Legists may come to discern more references to law in, and therefore seek more sources or influences for, Shakespeare's works from his life-text and law-texts. Furthermore, they might find a higher level of legal theory, more advanced political knowledge, and a greater complexity of juristic thought than has been hitherto anticipated. Critics may find that the "problem comedies" (i.e. *Merchant of Venice* and *Measure for Measure*) are less problematic and more coherent when they are perceived to concern specific and ornate legal issues. Biographers will hopefully find that many partial or thematic analyses and more complete biographical studies in Shakespeare can still be undertaken that connect the plays to his immediate concerns revealed in his life-text.

With *Measure for Measure* the level and content of Shakespeare's legal discourse becomes high indeed and of considerable significance. It reaches to the Crown and includes issues debated in the highest Courts.

Initially this discourse grew from his own law case involving inheritance, ultimately for his twin son. With his objectivity about how, like drama, law operates through language and interpretation, and his concern about crisis of intent through counter-intentionality, exercising the virtue of self-correction, he turns to having law do what he wants it to for his two daughters. In passing on the inheritance he bought it back for his father to his inheritors, entire. Thus he can use words to defeat the ravages of time.

Chapter V

His Daughters and Last Plays[1]

KENT.   Will you lie down and rest upon the cushions?
LEAR.   I'll see their [his daughters'] trial first. Bring in the
        evidence.
        [To Edgar] Thou robed man of justice, take thy place;
        [To the Fool] And thou, his yoke-fellow of equity,
        Bench by his side: [To Kent] you are o' the commission,
        Sit you too.
EDGAR. Let us deal justly.

King Lear. III.vi. 36-42

Shakespeare's autobiography enters his comedies *through* his court case and his twins. His play-texts enter into the context of the Inns of Court through contact with law-texts as well as twins. He discovers law issues by struggling with resolving his case, and when his son and heir dies, that event has an effect upon his plays at the Inns of Court. His law plays are selected for performance before the King at the beginning of his reign. As he comes closer to power he sees the power that influences law and how law can have the power he wants it to have to accomplish his desires in drama, at Court, and in life.

In retrospect the female line of inheritance always caused William Shakespeare some difficulty. His father had mortgaged away (see *Timon of Athens*) what was to have come to him from Mary, his mother. His only son, Hamlet (see *Hamlet*), had died at the age of eleven leaving his twin sister, Judith (*Twelfth Night*), and Susanna, an older sister conceived before wedlock (*Measure for Measure*), to be Shakespeare's only direct heirs. So for Shakespeare, his history plays, his final plays, his time and ours, inheritance important to the continuation of social structures was implicitly sex-linked through patrimony to male heirs. This chapter, using evidence from life-texts and law-texts in the play-texts, suggests that the preoccupation of Shakespeare with fathers and daughters in his last plays coincides with a similar concern evidenced in his life. His active desire to restore what his father lost through purchases to pass on to his male heir becomes legal activity to exercise his power of transmission through law language evidenced in the plays, and his law-texts, substantiate from his life Shakespeare's fear of betrayal in these matters as he tries to transfer his estate to his daughters. Perhaps we can also observe in this how the mechanism of societal inheritance travels along familial lines cut by paternalism. In Shakespeare's Jacobean tragedies, as we saw in *Hamlet*, and romances, as we saw in *The Merchant of Venice*, we find astonishing corroboration of life-text in Will's own story as the theme of land acquisition and conveyance is pursued through the process of inheritance from the point of view of the testator, William Shakespeare, as he personifies the central figure in *King Lear* and with Prospero in *The Tempest*. In the early plays, we watched victims manipulated by law and betrayed; now we see the dangers of betrayal from those who use and manipulate law and events against the passing on of inheritance and power.

In this later period, when Shakespeare puts a mirror up to the judicial process and mocks a court, as he does in *King Lear* (1605), he assumes it must represent the bifurcated fount of justice he has been advocating in his earlier comedies before King James and pursued previously in his personal cases in Queen's Bench and Chancery.

> LEAR.   I'll see their [his daughters', Gonoril's and Regan's]
> trial first. Bring in the evidence.
> [To Edgar] Thou robed man of justice, take thy place; [To
> the Fool] And thou, his yoke-fellow of equity,
> Bench by his side: [to Kent] you are o' the commission, Sit
> you too.
>
> (III.vi. 37-40)

A Commission is instituted with Justice and Equity, King's Bench and Chancery. The trial is set up by an old man for his two daughters.

King Lear, among other things, reveals Shakespeare's preoccupation at this time with justice and right due his authority and respect for his powers; an aging man's concern for his inheritance and passing it on to his offspring, with laws pertaining to these circumstances. The play-text can be read as the conjunction of Shakespeare's life-text and law-texts that he is reading at the time. His concern over the lack of male lineage is evidenced in the text of *Macbeth* (1606), in which Macbeth has no heirs and goes about killing the sons of others. Here too Duncan settles his inheritance in like manner as Claudius upon Hamlet (I.ii. 106-122);

> DUNCAN.
> Sons, kinsmen, thanes,
> And you whose places are the nearest, know
> We will establish our estate upon
> Our eldest, Malcolm, whom we name hereafter
> The Prince of Cumberland;
>
> (I.iv. 35-39)

With the death of his son and after the mourning of *Twelfth Night*, Shakespeare cannot establish his estate upon a male heir.

The dramatist evidences from advanced and recent legal language in the play-text of *Macbeth* his awareness of legal bonds and obligations between persons in the familiar "He's here in double trust;" (I.vii.12). Trusting or entrusting someone with an obligation is formalized by the legal act of establishing a trust, also known as the earlier "deed of gift." A trust is what Shakespeare will set up in order to ensure his estate will devolve upon his daughters, in hopes it will eventually be received by males of his own flesh.

Shakespeare devotes the initial part of the text of *Lear* to the legal action of a father dividing his estate among his daughters upon their marriages. When Lear does this, he discovers that his judgment has *betrayed himself* in the many senses in which we have been using the word. In his intent to be generous and produce love and happiness, the text produces the opposite, in so far as it reveals the fears lying behind the hand of a giver. The gift helps one to be free and happy but may find and cause evil. The giver may hope for the receiving generation to mature, suspecting it may abuse the opportunities. So Lear discovers his own betrayal through the legal texts' subsequent enactment; that he has brought forth by the laws of the body reinforced by the laws of inheritance, to which he has now made himself subject, daughters who become both the good and bad offspring. The play-text betrays other fears from the past imposed upon the future: that of the patrimony being stolen from the son in the subplot of Edmund's stealing the inheritance from his legitimate brother Edgar, recapitulating Shakespeare's experience of Edmund Lambert's holding from his brother-in-law (Shakespeare's father) what was to have been the dramatist's inheritance. Once again these autobiographical references (or intertextuality) to inheritance occur in initiating and motivating moments in main or subplot actions (as we have seen in *Macbeth*, *Hamlet*, to *As You Like It*, *Midsummer Night's Dream*, *Taming of the Shrew*, and loans and mortgages in *Merchant* and *Timon*, and twins in *Comedy* and *Twelfth Night*).

The root of evil in both plots in *King Lear* is sexual misconduct. The evil of Goneril and Regan is partly reflected in their sexual incontinence with Edmund. They show disrespect for their previous generation and their future ones. Edmund blames his evil upon his being Gloucester's natural son, an indictment of the problems in the transference of generation. Cordelia and Edgar are by contrast innocent, chaste, and true, despite legal text decisions against them. But are tragic victims of the folly of old men. The preoccupation on the part of Lear with his daughters can betray a deeper psychological problem beneath the legal transfer because they substitute for a wife and mother through these legal bonds of inheritance:

> LEAR. Tremble, thou wretch,
> That hast within thee undivulged crimes,
> Unwhipp'd of justice: Hide thee, thou bloody hand;
> Thou perjur'd, and thou simular of virtue,
> That art incestuous.
>
> (III.ii. 51-55)

Lear in attempting to endow his daughters for marriage is revealed as a father revered by the three daughters, then abused by two, and mothered by one.

In the very first scene of *King Lear*, the audience is witness to familial legal actions relating to inheritance. This is achieved by introducing law-text through pronouncement into the dramatic text. That is the obvious "intertextuality." Less obvious, but no less relevant to our concerns, is that the intertextuality comes from Shakespeare's life-text as well. Lear engages in the legal operations of the divestiture of property, the entailment of estate, the reservation in grant, and the construction of a dowry.[2] Documents, a legal text, bearing Shakespeare's fourth signature on law papers, show that in 1612 he confirms, in the Belott-Mountjoy suit, that he had participated on November 19, 1604 (the year before writing *King Lear*) in the setting up of a dowry by Christopher Mountjoy, his French Huguenot landlord who had property on a corner of Silver Street in London. Later Stephen Belott sued for the fulfillment of the dowry to accompany Mary Mountjoy. So once again, Shakespeare bore witness to the threatening of an inheritance another Mary (Mary Arden was his mother). Those were single dowries in legal texts; Shakespeare, we know from his life-text, is going to have to arrange for two in his immediate family; and Lear, in the play-text, handles three at once. All of these are threatened by a father's capacity and desire to withdraw, or alter the endowment, inheritance, or patrimony.

Thus *Lear* abounds in law, end-of-life concerns, sexual encounters, family, but chiefly reveals and betrays an old man and his idealized good and loyal daughter. These generalities are not distant from Shakespeare's own concerns at this time, as we have seen in other analogous moments in *Comedy* and *Twelfth Night*, but it will take further contextualizing from life and evidence of intertextuality to show how close. Mary Ellen Lamb warns that topicality and, by extension, references to life-text have been made loosely by critics in the past and have not offered insight into the creative process:

To what extent would Shakespeare have expected his audience to share his preoccupation? How much of the underlying context would they have been expected to 'get'? Would the names in this play have made them suspect a graver "point" somewhere, or would they have made the play even funnier?[3]

As she goes on to suggest, references may have been multiple: "Mary" may be a relative, or used generically, or merely with arbitrary specificity and at the same time. Legal references from his life obviously at the Inns coincided with professional and political concerns. She concludes that, while showing *Love's Labour's Lost* to be not necessarily grounded in coterie theatre, "I suspect that Shakespeare's plays are even more topical, more grounded in the social [and we may add, autobiographical] concerns of the day, than is now believed" (p. 59). The question of interest is how these personal problems become motives and how the fictions become resolutions for problems from the life-text. In his *Shakespeare's Romances and the Royal Family* David M. Bergeron raises the presence of the family and children in Shakespeare's plays:

> From our vantage point near the end of the twentieth century, it is exceedingly difficult to imagine what family life was like in the Middle Ages and the Renaissance. Yes, of course, we have evidence, but it is often contradictory. What were one's emotional ties to and feelings about other members of the family, however large or small that group might be? Fortunately, for our sake, a number of serious studies have been done on the history of the family. I find the work of Phillipe Aries and Lawrence Stone to be particularly valuable for my purposes; Aries emphasizes the centrality of the child, and Stone, the transient nature and patriarchal structure of the family. (p. 29)

Even more to our purposes, Bergeron continues to observe: "I think that Shakespeare's plays, especially the Romances, clearly reflect such an interest in children. These plays may be seen as 'speaking pictures' to join Aries's analysis of family portraits of the sixteenth and seventeenth centuries." (p. 29). In our case to even continue Shakespeare's synchronicity further, we would note that play-text may be interpenetrated at the same time by source and life-text. In other words, what better source for Shakespeare's portraits of Renaissance families but at times his very own?

In *Lear*, although Cordelia says she owes half her love to her father and half to her husband, Cordelia does return to console her father, Lear, in life and even goes to the extreme of joining him in death. This type of favoring is quite evident in Shakespeare's own personal life, culminating in the marriage of his eldest daughter

Susanna on June 5, 1607 to the brilliant Dr. John Hall, (in sharp contrast to her ostracized Grandfather, John Shakespeare), an accomplished and learned physician who resided in Stratford. Within the proper grace period was born a granddaughter christened Elizabeth Hall, on February 21, 1608 and likely being honored at some level of the text by Shakespeare in the passage on the birth of Queen Elizabeth in *Henry VIII* (1613):

```
KING.       What is her name?
CRANMER.    Elizabeth
            This royal infant — heaven still move about her: —
            Though in her cradle, yet now promises
            Upon this land a thousand thousand blessings...
                                              (V.v. 8-12)
```

In 1613 Shakespeare comes out of semi-retirement in Stratford to co-write the play referring to the monarch, 10 years dead, he grew up with and matured under. I cannot believe under those circumstances that there is not also a grandfatherly nod to his only granddaughter of the same name—the single offspring to pass on his blood to the generations to come.

In the same year following the birth of Elizabeth Hall Shakespeare's mother, Mary is buried on September 9, 1608. These events from the family history, denoting a general period in most families of near coincidence of births, deaths, and marriages of three generations, are clearly transferred from the life-text into play-text, often documented by intervening law-text. This we can discover in *Lear* (1605) with the marriage of his three daughters; the strange *Pericles* (1608) and its betrayal of an incestuous relationship between father and daughter and the problematic tragedy of *Coriolanus* (1608-1609), with Volumnia the mother dominating over the hero, at the time of Shakespeare's own mother's death. I am by no means *equating* figures in text with figures in, or from, life. Rather Shakespeare's mind, evidenced from the life-text, clearly is dominated by thoughts of his mother and mothers at the time of *Coriolanus*; about twins at the time of *Comedy of Errors*; about the death of fathers around *Hamlet*; of a twin son around *Twelfth Night*; and losses on failed payment of a bond around *Merchant of Venice*. From the evidence we can obviously go on to suggest that these autobiographical concerns of dowry, land losses, court case, twins, and inheritance appear through initial overt references, or intertextuality, in the very *first* scenes of *Lear, As You Like It, Merchant, Comedy, Midsummer, Hamlet, Taming,* and finally permeate the main character's concern and manipulations even in his last fully undisputed play—*The Tempest*.

The ambitious drives in Shakespeare, instilled by his father's rise and converted to retributive compensation by his father's fearful fall, were from the 1601 death of John Shakespeare onward redirected for and onto the women in Shakespeare's life. Possessing the patrimony from and to all in the family he was simultaneously son, husband, father, father-in-law and grandfather. One may look in the *Coriolanus* text for evidence of the struggle from the life-text necessitated by assuming these psychological and legal responsibilities, including his younger married sister and three unmarried brothers. One can note these fears concerning ambition and power projected upon women in his creations of Lady Macbeth (wife); Volumnia (mother); Cleopatra (mistress) and Goneril and Reagan (daughters). One can also find extreme innocence in the projected legal inheritors, Cordelia, Hermione, and Miranda. It is as if Shakespeare's counter-intentionalit y from what is occurring in his life-text is first being manifested and getting explored, then acted out, and finally studied in his play-texts.

Like Lear, Prospero in *The Tempest* has a daughter (Miranda) and no wife. The father projects his fear of sexual corruption of his offspring upon the character of the natural man, Caliban, and in *Lear* in Edmund, the natural son — both characters seek illegitimate relationships. This private tear and concomitant secret wish to protect and keep his daughters linked to his own desires, represented in Lear (patrimony) and Prospero (marriages), are carried to their explicit culmination in Pericles (incest) and Leontes of *The Winter's Tale*. Leontes' insane jealousy is anticipated in Othello, where his marriage causes the death of Brabantio, his father-in-law. This preoccupation with the female side of inheritance is portrayed in *Pericles* by the liaison between Antiochus and his daughter, and the characters of Thaisa, Marina, and their counterparts Dionyza, Lychorida (a nurse), and a Bawd presided over by Diana. With a similar pantheon of, in this case, virtuous women, *The Winter's Tale* presents the wife, Hermione, who is lost and returned upon the maturation of the daughter; Perdita, who is ready for marriage; Paulina, a spokeswoman for this wife-daughter complex of figures ranged against Leontes' jealousy. These plays, written when the males of Shakespeare's generation and his parents are dying around him, coincide with Shakespeare's mind turning from London's Court and the Inns of Court to Stratford, his pastoral fields, and residence, after the earlier loss of his only son, distantly echoed in Mamillius' death in *Winter's Tale*, to concentrate on his return to his wife, daughters, their marriages and offspring, in the way Leontes does in the same play. *Pericles* turns out to be an analysis of the father finding himself in his lost daughter-wife figures. *Coriolanus* is a study of a son's ambivalent feelings toward his mother, written following Shakespeare's own mother's death.

These personal preoccupations evidenced by the life-text are not devoid of legal-text representing sons possessing mothers' inheritance, as fathers transmit themselves to daughters, and husbands treat wives tyrannically in the play-texts. Along with these family portraits of the period in *Winter's Tale* (1610-1611), Shakespeare depicts a court trial perverted by the taint with which King James threatens Chancery in his assertion of royal prerogative. Coinciding with this emerging preoccupation with mothers, daughters, female innocence, mercy and equity, is Shakespeare's reservations about the willful and threatening justice figure of a father, a King, or a Leontes (lion) type. This preoccupation is converted in time from malevolence, to folly, to benignity, to benevolence in Claudius, Lear Leontes and Prospero, respectively, as Shakespeare ultimately handles this father figure in his art and, through his fiction, the types of these he is experiencing in life—his own father and King James, as well as himself. He knows that like law this figure can be self-serving, arbitrary, beneficent or cruel. Like drama, law and powerful figures are best when just, precise, and properly motivated toward edification, clarity, and compassion.

At this stage in Shakespeare's public and personal career, we know from Thomas Greene's letters, which indicate he is about to move out of New Place in 1610, that he plans to return to Stratford and his family. In this pastoral town far from London, he turns his attention to his second daughter, Judith. *The Tempest* text presents a former Duke exercising his magic by which the world is brought to admire his daughter, the wife-mother absent, protecting Miranda from Caliban and bestowing her upon a Prince. Many of these elements from the later play-texts turn out surprisingly to have also synchronicity with events in the life-text. Whereas the earlier plays respond to the life elements, toward the end Shakespeare's concerns in the play-texts reappear *subsequently* in the life-text. The process seems to reverse itself; for texts that is possible. But we must avoid assuming his plays affect his life causally; that would be absurdly simplistic. Just as we have previously avoided arguing that his plays are descriptions of his life, we now must not presume he learns from, extends, or reacts to his own plays. However, there is a connection. He does consider problems related to his concern for his daughters and inheritance, and some of these dramatizations of his options or betrayals of his fears and hopes do take place. His interests in his daughters as exhibited in his art and play-texts are met with manifestations of these fears from the real world, evidenced from subsequent life-texts, in sexual slanders upon his favored daughter and sexual corruption encountered by his less-favored daughter. Both events are revealed in law-texts, dramatized by court action in suits (Schoenbaum, *Compact Documentary Life*, pp. 289-290, 293-294).

As has been observed, Shakespeare's eldest daughter Susanna is married on June 5, 1607 to John Hall, a learned man, a distinguished physician, and a noted citizen. Scandal erupts in the Hall household in 1613. As a consequence on July 13 Susanna seeks a writ of slander and brings action for defamation (cf. *Measure for Measure*, II.i. 190) in the Consistory, an Ecclesiastical Court at Worcester. Susanna's charge is against John Lane. His uncle is Richard Lane. Shakespeare had asked Richard to be one of the witnesses for the Commission out of Chancery on the Lambert controversy, through which Shakespeare lost his mother's inheritance finally in 1599. He was also of the Shakespeare party in the suit to Chancery on the Stratford tithes during the dramatist's retirement. John Lane (Jr.) had earlier accused Shakespeare's eldest daughter by claiming that Susanna "...had the running of the reins and had been naught [i.e. immoral] with Rafe Smith at John Palmer [a small town]." Ralph Smith is a Stratford haberdasher and hatter; his uncle is none other than Hamlet Sadler, the close friend and baker neighbor of Shakespeare (for whom, as Godfather, Shakespeare named his son). The males of the second generation of close acquaintances are a threat to the reputation of his daughters; and in the case of Judith to come, and at first Susanna, the Shakespeares strike back at the male contemporaries of the son William no longer had.

With this court case, the legal-text makes Susanna from the life-text subject to precisely the slanderous, unfounded accusation of adultery Shakespeare has Leontes in his earlier play-text direct at Hermione in *Winter's Tale*. John Lane, "...a ne'er -do-well, was some years later hauled into court for riot and libels against the vicar and aldermen, and was then described as a drunkard."[4] Robert Whatcott is the lawyer who represents Mrs. Susanna Shakespeare Hall and is often not recognized, or is misidentified, by scholars and critics when they encounter his name as one of the witnesses of Shakespeare's Last Will and Testament. Robert Whatcott is another one of the numerous attorneys or representatives working for, or associated with, the Shakespeare family (Greene, Overbury, Powle, Stovell, etc.). John Lane did not appear in court to support the rumors he had spread and was excommunicated. Shakespeare's family's use of law sent the nephew of a friend to Hell! Susanna's valued chastity had been maligned, but like the play-text Hermione, the law-text in life shows she survived the accusation triumphantly, and like Cordelia is ultimately honored by her father, receiving New Place and virtually all his personal property upon his death. The Will is a dramatic law-text in the life-text, indeed, possibly authored by the dramatist. Susanna's epitaph upon her tomb after she dies in 1649 reads:

> Witty above her sex, but that's not all,
> Wise to salvation was good Mistress Hall;
> Something of Shakespeare was in that, but this
> Wholly of him with whom she's now in bliss.
>
> (*Ibid.*, p. 7)

So, as he had desired, something of himself had been preserved against the slings and arrows of outrageous fortune. And, like Cordelia, Susanna joins her father in death as suggested by the writer of this funereal text, becoming the inheritor of God's kingdom too.

Both daughters cause Shakespeare concern during his retirement. On February 10, 1616, when she is nearly 31, Judith, the younger daughter of Shakespeare, marries Thomas Quiney, the son of Shakespeare's friend Richard Quiney and grandson of John Shakespeare's companion Adrian. Thomas was a vintner, or innkeeper, and is 26 at the time, much Judith's junior, reminiscent of Will's marriage. Perhaps Judith had tried to please her father and later even names her son "Shaxper." Unfortunately he dies in infancy. Fate is against her. Anthony Burgess narrates the development of the situation well:

> Marriage to a tavern-keeper was scarcely what Will would have chosen for his younger daughter, especially as it was—like his own—a marriage conducted in suspicious haste. The haste is attested by the fact that February 10 came within the period for special licences. The special licence that had been obtained for Will and Anne, all those years before, had been obtained in a regular manner and from the Stratford vicar, and apparently this was so irregular that he (and not, as would have been just, the vicar) was summoned to the consistory court at Worcester. He (like John Lane before) refused to go, or forgot, and was fined and excommunicated. This was not a very good start to the state of holy matrimony.[5]

Unfortunately Thomas' sexual activity had met with several successes in close proximity. A certain Margaret Wheeler had become pregnant by Quiney nine months before, and the sexual misconduct suddenly becomes evident to society a month after his marriage to the pregnant Judith. Quiney must have reminded Shakespeare of his characterization of Angelo in *Measure for Measure* and Bertrand in *All's Well That Ends Well* but, fortunately, in the play-text Shakespeare can suddenly switch their nearly adulterous designs to their betrothed at the last moments.

Wheeler and the child die and are buried on the Ides of March (15th) 1616. On March 26th, with the lawyer Thomas Greene, Will's cousin and former lodger, as prosecuting counsel, Quiney confesses in court that he has had "carnal intercourse with the said Wheeler" and is sorry. He has good reason for being genuinely sorry, for the day before the trial, Shakespeare alters his will drastically, much reducing poor Judith's expectations. She is inadvertently punished for her match. Thomas has to do public penance (something Henry IV does not live to do). Thomas Quiney was ordered to and did appear in William Shakespeare's Trinity Parish Church on three successive Sundays. By the end of the period of contrition for his betrayal, the great dramatist, Thomas' father-in-law, William Shakespeare is dead! All life-, law- and play-texts end.

Thomas had married into the Shakespeare family without producing his share of the marriage settlement of one hundred pounds in land. Later, he was to be fined for swearing and for allowing drunkenness on his premises.[6] The episode of Judith, as well as that of Susanna, evidences that the play-texts of the later period, his late tragedies and romances, do relate to and anticipate the life-texts of his retirement. They initially evidence a fear of betrayal in the father, or counter-intentionality on his part toward his recipients, that approaches tyranny as opposed to a free gift from love, which while explored and handled by the genre form of the art, in turn manifests itself in the life-text in the form of threats from offspring of contemporary friends fortunate to have surviving sons, but not of fortunate character.

Shakespeare ends his fiction with appropriate denouements of tragic, comic and romance drama but he also constructs through law-texts the denouements for his opposition in life. Both use words and systems of rules to bring about their judgments and resolutions. The Shakespeares took up the law to protect themselves, to punish and reward at a time when the dramatist was personally reenacting the tragedy (life-text mirroring play-text) of the good and evil daughters of *King Lear* and reexperiencing a mood toward daughters captured in the adulterous slander of *Winter's Tale*. Earlier parts of the life-text are introduced into his play-texts by Shakespeare and now looking back over the play-texts he sees them manifested in his life-text. Clearly he must have felt a grandfatherly wisdom, not only having seen it all before but having been there before in the fiction sprung from his intents and counter-intents. Striking of these, especially in regard to Thomas and his daughter Judith, must have been the sexual theatre in *The Tempest*:

PROSPERO.
> Then, as my gift and thine own acquisition
> Worthily purchased, take my daughter; but
> If thou doest break her virgin-knot before
> All sanctimonious ceremonies may
> With full and holy rite be minister'd
> No sweet aspersion shall the heavens let fall
> To make this contract grow; but barren hate,
> Sour-eyed disdain and discord shall bestrew
> The union of your bed with weeds as loathly
> That you shall hate it both.

(IV.i. 13-22)

Inheritance carries implicit assumptions about chastity. Chastity preserves inheritance from the father through the child to offspring to come within the family name or through daughters' blood lines. To disturb this is "evil" in the family, society, and among offspring. A son may die but a daughter can be tossed into utter darkness by disinheritance and the offending male by excommunication.

Evil, particularly with sexual overtones, corrupted metaphysically in the art but then for Shakespeare it erupts into reality. The tyranny of the law is invoked to produce punishment, vindication, reward, and the casting away of the unruly sons (play-text Caliban and Edmund; life-text John Lane and Thomas Quiney). Patrimony is attacked by the ignorant, unknowing, and false accusing (Lane and Edmund figures) and the unconscious, willful, and beastly (Quiney and Caliban figures) again in life, and close to the end. Had it hastened the end? Signatures on the Will indicate that Shakespeare went fast. Judith's marriage is in February; Quiney's trial is in March; and Shakespeare is dead in April 1616. Many of his fictional fears had been realized and the blows had come across the generation from sons of friends. But his legacy survived—he may not have known his play-texts would—with judicious alterations of law-text. Shakespeare's estate was to have gone to his son Hamlet. He protected his daughters so that they would receive it by legal means. He removed all but a silver bowl for Thomas Quiney after his trial; instead of a dowry and property and portions of the estate for her male offspring, Judith saw it all shifted to Susanna. This was so that Judith's Thomas would get nothing, and only if she divorced him would receive anything and then only cash. Thus through law his intent was directed to Susanna and counter-intentionality to Judith, keeping his entire estate intact for some future male heir ("seventh issue ensuing male") by the reach of law. This is the kind of will produced by Portia's dead father in *Merchant*. In the form of deed of gift or "trust" to Susanna and John Hall one sees the same inheritance that Jessica receives in the same play. Indeed, he had seen his life-text before in his own play-text in analogous law-texts and constructions, or "symboleography", as the law theorists called it.

If Shakespeare's death were not hastened by difficulties over his daughter's inheritance, at least his plays corroborate a preoccupation with this subject. He felt he was under social pressure to make a good end upon his family. The difficulty of doing this presents a particular problem for Shakespeare. The law of primogeniture runs against his blood circumstances, with two female heirs inheriting through their husbands. With the sexual bias of the law against women interfering with their direct reception of their father's devotion or grandparents' love, we can witness in the life records and the plays a conjunction of concerns and problems Shakespeare has to face. In the case of Shakespeare, despite his knowledge of the tragedy of King Lear and Cordelia and happy resolution of Prospero and Miranda, he had to be inequitable to Judith, his younger daughter and twin of his only son, and give all to Susanna. ("'Poor dear,'" quoth he, 'thou makest a testament/As worldings do, giving thy sum of more/To that which had too much: '" (*As You Like It*. II.i. 47-49.) One of the wealthiest men in Stratford had to disinherit one of his daughters to protect his estate from her husband. There is play-text and law-text in his life-text as evidence that he was not pleased at all about having to do so.

So the later plays shift their text as Shakespeare's life-text indicates law-text preoccupations with the mother and daughter figures in his life. As in the earlier plays we witness crossovers between his configuration of characters in plays and law language in documents in his life. Even as the earlier blank years come alive from law-text, so his silent "retirement' years are no longer quiet, nor any less relevant to his play-texts. As his play-texts develop, more of his personal problems become evident in legal and political areas. Sophistication and "play" enter not only the deeper realms of psychological compensation and wish-fulfillment, but as the stories become more "fantastic" the psychological narration of dramatized betrayal of counter-intentionality becomes more accurate and "realistic". We may then see how a play does not become "prophetic", or life an enactment, of a previously conscious text. Rather, as Shakespeare becomes more familiar with his own, and man and woman's depths, he can bring more of one's complete self to the surface: the suppressed, contrarities, and conflicting synchronicities together. As we have seen, by placing his personal concerns at the very beginnings of plays, he can observe them moving from his present to his future with double results—gains and losses, tragedies and comedies, deaths and returns, good and bad daughters, success and failure of inheritances, hope and despair of human values and continuities. It takes time for us and Shakespeare to realize or manifest this phenomenon. However, in retrospect it is present even in its earliest forms: a father-in-law dies of a broken heart in *Othello*. Even the first appearance of fictive twins in *Comedy* when his are both alive in life, is about a father searching for them who seem to be as lost as Sebastian is to be in *Twelfth Night*. Hamlet will be lost forever in reality.

Chapter VI

Life-Text in Play-Text

FERDINAND.
>This is a most majestic vision, and
>Harmonious charmingly. May I be bold
>To think these spirits?

PROSPERO.
>Spirits, which by mine art
>I have from their confines call'd to enact
>My present fancies.

FERDINAND.
>Let me live here ever;
>So rare a wonder'd father and a wife
>Makes this place Paradise.
>[Juno and Ceres whisper, and send Iris on employment.]

PROSPERO.
>Sweet, now, silence!
>Juno and Ceres whisper seriously;
>There's something else to do: hush, and be mute,
>Or else our spell is marr'd.

IRIS.
>You nymphs, call'd Naiads, of the wandring brooks,
>With your sedged crowns and ever-harmless looks,
>Leave your crisp channels and on this green land
>Answer your summons; Juno does command:
>Come, temperate nymphs, and help to celebrate
>A contract of true love; be not too late.

Enter certain Nymphs.

>You sunburnt sicklemen, of August weary,
>Come hither from the furrow and be merry:
>Make holiday; your rye-straw hats put on
>And these fresh nymphs encounter every one
>In country footing.

Enter certain Reapers, properly habited: they join with the Nymphs in a graceful dance; towards the end whereof Prospero starts suddenly, and speaks; after which, to a strange, hollow, and confused noise, they heavily vanish.

PROSPERO.
>[Aside] I had forgot that foul conspiracy
>Of the beast Caliban and his confederates
>Against my life: the minute of their plot
>Is almost come. [To the Spirits] Well done! avoid;
>no more!

FERDINAND.
>This is strange: your father's in some passion
>That works him strongly.

MIRANDA.
> Never till this day
> Saw I him touch'd with anger so distemper'd
PROSPERO.
> You do look, my son, in a moved sort,
> As if you were dismay'd: be cheerful, sir.
> Our revels now are ended. These our actors,
> As I foretold you, were all spirits and
> Are melted into air, into thin air:
> And, like the baseless fabric of this vision,
> The cloud-capp'd towers [of London], the gorgeous palaces,
>   [Whitehall, Greenwich]
> The solemn [middle and inner] temples, the great globe itself,
> Yea, all which it inherit, shall dissolve
> And, like this insubstantial pageant faded,
> Leave not a rack behind. We are such stuff
> As dreams are made on, and our little life
> Is rounded with a sleep. Sir, I am vex'd;
> Bear with my weakness; my old brain is troubled:
> Be not disturb'd with my infirmity:
> If you be pleased, retire into my cell
> And there repose: a turn or two I'll walk,
> To still my beating mind.
FER./MIRANDA.
> We wish your peace. [Exeunt.]
PROSPERO.
> Come with a thought. I thank thee, Ariel: come.

Enter Ariel.

ARIEL.
> Thy thoughts I cleave to. What's thy pleasure?
PROSPERO.
> Spirit,
> We must prepare to meet with Caliban.
ARIEL.
> Ay, my commander: when I presented Ceres,
> I thought to have told thee of it, but I fear'd
> Lest I might anger thee.
>   *The Tempest* IV.i. 117-169

The obvious implication of this study is that no one can claim any longer Shakespeare's plays do not contain direct autobiographical elements. The relationships of life-text and play-texts are now open for vast and varied critical investigation in a manner analogous to source study, good topical analysis, and psychological speculation. Furthermore these connections prove for the popular reader that the author is the man from Stratford, who knew and was fascinated by many aspects of English law, most of which appear also in his life-text. We know a lot more not only about him but how his plays were conceived or designed with some retrievable "intentionality" and "counter-intentionality. " More specifically, we can reconstruct more about his "blank" years of 1585-1595, and also his "retirement" 1610-1616. Schoenbaum's texts from Shakespeare's life records can be used as a "source", as supporting or analogous materials along with the play-texts for even more revelations. The Man Shakespeare stands before us perhaps never to be a complete portrait but like Picasso's portraits a holograph version in which we can discern many legitimate faces, realizing that these are all constructs and some self-fashionings. However, this leaves a lot of exciting things to see and do. In addition, productions can underscore or connect these concerns in theatrically interesting ways. Some of our methodology may enable critics to apply methods to the inner horizons of Shakespeare, and Shakespeare studies in turn can validate criticism producing valuable and perceptive results in the realm of outer horizons to his work.

This new evidence suggests, especially in the area of equity, that Shakespeare was neither a political nor historical conservative. As borne out by accomplishments, which include the performance of the plays before jurists and his connections with legal history, Shakespeare was on the contrary a radical "futurist," prophesying events in his private life (*Lear* and his daughters) and anticipating and influencing changes in English laws pertaining to equity. More interesting is to realize how closely in tune he was to his own life's psychological, legal, and familial developments by working them through in his play-texts.

As has been seen, much is known about Shakespeare, and if ordered as we have thematically (heirs and inheritance) from the legal documents (law-texts), the dramas (play-texts) and biography (life-text), much more significant information can be discerned about the author when these areas impinge upon each other (intertextually). This new data can change the predominant attitude amongst writers, critics, and biographers about his authorship, the nature of his mind, the scope of his intellect, the depth of his interests, and the relevance of his active concern about his family and law and equity. His social and political involvement was felt in law, at Court, through the Theatre, in Estates, and at the Inns of Court. Shakespeare's legal background moves from personal motives to profound judicial considerations before the highest judges and courts. He was not necessarily trying to influence but certainly to inform the audience, sometimes including the King, about difficult and complex current legal debates, issues or points at law, particularly if in conflict with equity jurisdictions.

I, reluctantly offer an *astounding* possibility. The more I looked into these "autobiographical" elements the more it was noted that they seem to *instigate* main and/or subplots. Perhaps the reader might accept from the accumulated evidence that possibly Shakespeare selected certain plots because they were analogous to his own experiences and actually began writing from personal experience. In *Hamlet* and *As You Like It*, we find a frame. In *Comedy* and *Twelfth Night* the autobiographical elements pervade the plot. In *Taming* his explicit reference to his uncle gets him started and he goes onto other things. In *Lear* his personal concerns begin both plots and he travels into the very depths and resolutions of these issues so as to explore both their positive and negative results. *Measure for Measure* may explore the very ambiguities of examining one's own intents to offer wish-fulfillments or self-revelations. Thus betraying the action as attempts at finding substitutions. Laws as well as plays may be beneficent, or reveal tyranny. They can condemn people, and they can reward. These texts are ultimately merely words, but they are things kings take very seriously.

In addition to the living monuments of his plays, Shakespeare participated in legally historical developments, which were passed on to following generations. His offspring, legal-texts and dramatic-texts were inheritors of his life, legal actions, and plays, particularly when these areas intersected. He enacted his part at the very moment English law was making major contributions of equity to the Anglo-American legal heritage (in contradistinction to Continental and Roman law). *Shakespeare v. Lambert* contributed to the concept of equity of redemption, enjoyed now as grace periods for mortgages and loans. Sustaining Chancery by his bifurcated presentation of law in his plays before the King contributed to preservation of equity of a statute, which is one of the chief interpretive functions of the Supreme Court (with Chancellor Ellesmere's jurisdiction being the British analogy). It is clear that many of Shakespeare's plays before King James, during the controversial 1603-1616 period determining supremacy, continuously depicted (*Comedy, Merchant, Measure, Lear*) the supremacy of equity over common law, which is enjoyed in the notion of an appellate court system and rights of appeal, as Bacon's Commission wrote on behalf of James. Through his plays, Shakespeare not only made the intricacy of law available to lower levels of his audience but by his productions and legal actions dramatized its problems and explored tough implications in its very nature.

After a life of being in and at law; of imitating precisely and at high levels his life-text and its law-texts in his play-texts; of acquiring properties by the law; Shakespeare finally transmits his acquirements through the law in his own Last Will and Testament (also in his own hand?):[1]

> ...the said premisses to be & Remaine to my sayed Neece Hall [Elizabeth, granddaughter]...
> To have & to hold All & singular the saied
> premisses with their Appurtennaunces unto
> the saied Susanna Hall...Item I Gyve
> & bequeth unto my daughter Judyth [Shakespeare
> had first put down 'sonne,' added an L'
> and then crossed it out, so he was thinking
> of a son at the very last, in the last piece of
> surviving writing he engaged in.] One Hundred & ffiftie pounds of lawfull English money...Item I gyve unto my wief [Anne Hathaway] my second best bed with the furniture...& the ffiftie Poundes to be sett fourth by my executours during the lief of my Sister Johane Harte...

Shakespeare had worked to re-establish his father's estate, and in turn the women in Shakespeare's life, who had been deprived of their possession by John Shakespeare, received its expanded substitute (earned from his fictions) from William. William had fixed on the authority figure of his father, the High Bailiff, the Justice, the judge (some had thought him a Butcher and Will a Butcher's son), and William had seen him rob his mother and himself of her inheritance by his decline.

This wisdom from his father's losses (depicted in *Timon*) went into his text in *King Lear*:

FOOL.   Sirrah, I'll teach thee a speech.
LEAR.   Do.
FOOL.   Mark it nuncle:
            Have more than thou showest,
            Speak less than thou knowest,
            And lend less than thou owest,
            Ride more than thou goest,
            Learn more than thou throwest;
            Leave thy drink and thy whore
            And keep in-a-door,
            And thou shall have more
            Than two tens to a score.
KENT.   This is nothing, fool.
FOOL.   Then 'tis like the breath of an unfee'd lawyer;
            You gave me nothing for 't. Can you make no
            use of nothing, nuncle.
LEAR.   Why, no, boy; nothing can be made out of nothing.
FOOL.   [To Kent] Prithee, tell him, so much the rent of
            His land comes to: he will not believe a fool.
LEAR.   A bitter fool!
FOOL.   Dost thou know the difference, my boy, between
            A bitter fool and a sweet fool?
LEAR.   No, lad; teach me.

```
FOOL.        That lord that counsell'd thee
             To give away thy land,
             Come place him here by me,
             Do thou for him stand:
             The sweet and bitter fool
             Will presently appear;
             The one in motley here,
             The other found out there.
LEAR.        Dost thou call me fool, boy?
FOOL.        All thy other titles thou hast given away;
             That thou wast born with.
KENT.        This is not altogether fool, my lord.
```

(I.iv. 128-165)

The Fool has learned much from John Shakespeare's failures and Will's successes. Shakespeare worked to build his father up, and surpass his reputation in order to overcome him and the self-destructive tendency in him he feared. He had handled the desires and fears associated with butchering this figure in his studies of Caesar, Claudius, Duncan, Macbeth, Hamlet, Brutus, from his revenge and history plays (like *Titus Andronicus* and *Richard III*). Hamlet the avenger for justice had died in the play, as well as in the son. Shakespeare would gentle his own condition; Will would become the son of a gentleman, by making his father a gentleman. However, what had been allied with the Justice was Mary, a mercy figure, at first deprived but ultimately coming to the fore and surviving the male, as all the women did their men (e.g. Joan, Anne, Judith, Susanna, and Elizabeth). Likewise in the latter plays, synchronicity with Shakespeare's later life-text, the female mercy-figure triumphs over the male folly of giving away lands or dispensing rigorous and harsh justice. As fate would have it Shakespeare shared his actual inheritance (Henley Street House) from his father with his mother and, symbolically, finally only received it clear from her upon her death. He promptly passed it on to be enjoyed by his ultimately widowed sister for nominal rent (and it is her lineage that survives to this day). All his possessions went to the surviving Anne, Judith (in abeyance), and, of course, Susanna, and her Elizabeth.

His granddaughter Elizabeth was for Shakespeare a phoenix for the dead Queen, who without an immediate issue, or heir, had been replaced by the tyrannical King James, who had threatened Chancery and equity. The dramatist repeatedly represented these concepts without reprimand. In fact with repeated command performance (*Merchant*), the King allowed them to survive in Bacon's Commission. The infant Elizabeth had been personified and sometimes anticipated in the plays by Miranda, Perdita, Cordelia, Isabella, Portia, and

Desdemona. Shakespeare in this brave new world would have Good grow with her, as he eulogized the little princess in his last play:

> In her days every man shall eat in safety
> Under his own vine, what he plants; and sing
> The merry songs of peace to all his neighbors:
> ...peace, plenty, love, truth, terror.

The fear of loss is still there at the end, but it is in awe of such dreamed of innocence, goodness, and mercy he has brought about in his life's work of propagation and preservation, of artistic and legal accomplishments associated with the Inns of Court. An even greater sense of what is right through equity, as he learned in his suits in Chancery, became one of Shakespeare's many legacies to human consciousness: "our children's children/Shall see this, and bless heaven", as he had said at the end of his last play.

Shakespeare learned much about the law. What it ultimately taught him to realize about his own life was that justice, in father and king figures, was not what he was after, or they betrayed and threatened him. The much more apparently vulnerable, nevertheless, finally prevailing equity in mother-, mercy-figures was to transmit his particular legacy. The loop between Shakespeare's life-text and play-texts is circular, particularly through conjunction of law-texts, so that all are interrelated. Perceptions from drama may have led to additional legal actions and legal actions may have produced some of the plays or at least certain dramatic moments. Of this there can no longer be any doubt. It is surprising that we ever thought Shakespeare was not in his plays, or that there was no way to determine that fact; or that it would have useless, or uninteresting results.

Shakespeare's depiction of the Fool in *Lear* as the judge of equity indicates he is not alone in what was happening in drama and law in the English Renaissance, and that he was also participating in events of a period that would come to a crisis after his death. After Ben Jonson's *Bartholomew Fair* (1610), the legal representatives in Jonson's plays become fools and crooks. The judge in *The Devil is an Ass* (1616) is named Justice Eitherside, and in *The Staple of News* (1625) is Picklock. In the latter play the judicial process (as it is in *Lear*) is mocked by an old man carrying out a mad trial with his dogs. Under the influence of Elizabeth, Shakespeare portrayed justice as seasoned with divine mercy and even a thought of Christ. Under the reign of James I, which included the 1621 impeachment of the Chancellor, Sir Francis Bacon for bribery, the justice figures in the play-texts fail to operate because the late play of Ben Jonson has an eye on "Adam" and man's frailty in *Justice Overdo*.

With his moral voice thus theatrically undermined, *Bartholomew Fair* is Jonson's last great comedy and bespoke the end of moral comedy until after the Restoration. Both Jonson and Shakespeare had vied for performances at the Inns of Court in the 1590's. Jonson died in 1637, three years before the closing of the theaters by Parliament in 1641, when

> ...the Puritans won their sixty years' war
> with the dramatists and closed the theatres.
> In honesty, it must be confessed that they
> silenced no voice of great importance.[2]

Within the year, the Long Parliament dissolved the prerogative courts and the Court of Star Chamber because of its vindictive punishments and associations with despotic rule under the Stuarts. Chancery received the power of equity when it finally hardened into the ruled common law procedures of modern England, after reforms and amalgamation of the bifurcated system in Victorian times. Dickens' *Bleak House* was a popularization of Chancery problems, prompting that Court to be assimilated into the single Crown court system.

The institutions of drama and prerogative law had become corrupt by the beginning of the reign of Charles I (1625). By acts of Parliament, the Puritans (burlesqued by Shakespeare in Malvolio of *Twelfth Night*), with the support of serious critics of the drama and the jurists of the period, abolished the theaters and Star Chamber. By doing so, they closed the two secular avenues that had explicitly expressed the concept of Divine mercy through the principle of equity, even after the Reformation. Before their end, each institution had given a voice to its predicament delivered by one of their number. In the drama Justice Overdo in Jonson's *Bartholomew Fair* is criticized for his frailty and lack of authority and responds:

> They may have seen many a fool in the
> habit of a Justice; but never till now, a
> Justice in the habit of a fool.[3]

The jurist John Selden (1584-1654) voices his criticism of the jurisprudence of the period:

> Equity is a roguish thing. For law we have
> a measure, know what to trust to; Equity
> is according to the conscience of him that
> is Chancellor, and as that is larger or

narrower, so is Equity. 'Tis all one as if
they should make the standard for the
measure we call a "foot" a Chancellor's
foot; what an uncertain measure would
this be! One Chancellor has a long foot,
another a short foot, a third an indifferent
foot. 'Tis the same thing in the Chancellor's
conscience.

(Table Talk)

The Puritans' demand for absolute rational and moral authority in the
human realm points up the lack of it in society; they close the theaters,
abolish the Star Chamber, and kill the King.

In *Bartholomew Fair* and the words of John Selden, voicing an
opposing opinion to Shakespeare's productions before James (1602-
1616), we hear one result of the Reformation--the basic assumption of
the relativistic nature of human authority. When in the drama the
Mercy-figure and in jurisprudence the Chancellor, whose authority was
undisputed in the fifteenth century, are after the Reformation seen as
subject to frailty, arbitrariness and uncertainty, then the principles of
equity cease to be related to Divine mercy and grace. When at the time
William Perkins, a Puritan theologian "...and the other divines were
faced with clear violations, in the common law, of God's scriptural law
or of Christian equity as they understood it, they invariably engaged in
rather shocking casuistry to defend the common law" (Hill, 81-82). It
was Perkins who had said there was "good reason then that lawyers
take the Divines' advice, touching Equitie, which is the intent of the
law," but he had found one kind of man reprehensible: "...such...(as by a
certain foolish kinde of pitty, are so carried away), that would have
nothing but mercie, mercie..." Just as critics are not supposed to discover
the intent of Shakespeare's text (the author is dead), it is precisely the
intent of law-texts that equity which Shakespeare was so fascinated
by, is designed to discover, particularly in *Measure for Measure*.

In the face of rigorous and harsh justice, we have seen Shakespeare's drama from 1594 to 1610 presenting alternative mercy in
theology and equity in law; and in turn, we observe that his dramas
borrowed the legal concept of equity to resolve plot situations by
introducing a higher, but more arbitrary, system of law in *Comedy*,
Merchant and *Measure for Measure*, and referred to as a mock device in
Lear.

In politics, law, and literature, this highly just but arbitrary
concept of equity was defended by Shakespeare, Bacon, Ellesmere,
Lambarde, Hooker, and other natural law and Chancery apologists
who often had to appeal to abstractions and ultimate mysteries of

divine grace. Ben Jonson, Coke, Perkins, Selden and other Puritanical divines and jurists complained about the aristocratic tyranny associated with equity's privileged administration, proclaiming instead the necessity of predictable, unvarying human written law to meet the totality of human failings. To accomplish seeming equality, rather than equity before the law, became the aim of justice, which ignored exceptions rather than having law achieve exceptional justice. Legal historians would admit that with Ellesmere and Lambarde, Chancery, in its long history, had achieved one brief shining moment that coincided with its reflection in Shakespeare's depiction of it from 1588 to 1616. We have witnessed through examination of legal-texts, play-texts, and life-texts of Shakespeare from 1570 to 1640 the awareness, the mirroring, the anatomization and the decline of English equity in law and drama, Chancery and society, as Shakespeare encountered it. What is so remarkable is that Shakespeare's drama should reflect this so directly and explicitly, serving as a running commentary upon it with such direct personal involvement, precise awareness, and sustained concern as well as penetrating theoretical analysis. Edmund Spenser, then a Clerk of Chancery in Ireland, seems in Book V of *The Faerie Queene* to have presented equity in literature with the most explicit awareness of its technical delicacy, glory and hazards. Shakespeare knows of it in his early plays, assumes it in *Comedy of Errors*, discloses its beneficial arbitrariness in *Merchant of Venice*, and discovers its harmful social implications in *Measure for Measure*. But he ultimately maintains his faith in its theological base. That base had been conveyed from late Medieval drama's uses of the female mercy-figure (daughter of God type) to Shakespeare's time via the Interludes (referred to in Shakespeare's *Henry VIII*) and their comic justice figures dispensing equity.

Shakespeare, Lambarde and Spenser display the institutionaliza-tion of equity in their courts as had Aeschylus in the *Oresteia* (Court of Aereopagus). The medieval Macro plays (*Castle of Perseverance* and *Mankynde*) dramatize the presence of equity by name, as had Homer at the end of the *Odyessy* by his use of Athene. Ben Jonson and Jacobean legal and theological writers had observed and even welcomed the demise of the concept, as its absence had been analyzed by Sophocles in *Antigone*. The Puritans and letter-of-the-law people (Coke and King's Bench justices) did away with mercy, grace, equity, arbitrariness and interpretation by their new law codes, theology, doctrine of the elect, which at the same time seeks to suppress art forms that dramatize these alternative human or divine avenues of behavior. The study of drama can tell us something about the society it reflects. By discerning with precision and sometimes surprising immediacy how the concept of equity from legal thought is being used in the drama at any given time, perhaps there are clues in the theater, not only to an individual author's personal interests, but what the interest of the period appears to be toward in its own law and authority figures. Looking at law in drama over a period of time discloses equity as one of the most abstract, sometimes arbitrary, often fragile, but most sought-after of the "goods" or higher values in humanity. Opposite absolute law there stands the greater ideal of absolute justice.

Shakespearean criticism is not written for the man on the street, even one who goes to the plays. Legal theory and history are not even many lawyers' favorite topics. But when these coincide to produce startlingly serious and interesting points about Shakespeare himself, newspapers, students, colleagues, seat companions on planes, trains and buses turn to hear. I believe this data is neither surmise nor conjecture, nor will essentially be completely supplanted by some new information. Undeniably, Shakespeare refers to himself and his life in his plays: his twins in *Comedy* and *Twelfth Night*; his son in *King John* and *Hamlet*; his daughters marriageability and dowries in *Lear* and *Tempest*; his sexual relationship with his wife before marriage in *Measure for Measure*; Lambert in *Taming* and *Lear*; his court case in *As You Like It* and *Merchant*; losing land in *As You Like It* and *Hamlet*; his father's financial difficulties in *Timon* and *Dream*; the loss of his son in *Twelfth Night* and *Macbeth*. These are only the obvious examples.

They become more than momentary passing references, however, when seen to refer to the one specific court case from *Comedy* to *Lear* dealing with his inheritance; refer to the loss of his male heir from *King John* to *Macbeth*; to refer to twins and double dowries from *Comedy* to *Lear* and passing on his estates to his daughters from *Lear* to *Tempest*. Then there is a barrage of "legal" plays before "legal" audiences at the Inns and at Court on these issues: *Comedy*, *Merchant*, *Twelfth Night* and *Measure*. On the other hand this would have been all too obvious from the beginning and would make this book unnecessary if Shakespeare's references had been overbearing or not assimilable into general meanings. None of the references require personal explication to convey their immediate meaning. None of the plays or characters become totally absorbed in these particular concerns. However, when the entire works are seen as a single text, the mapping of these references becomes quite revealing.

They turn out to have significant placement. They begin action as if Shakespeare has to use a key personal psychological moment to get his text rolling. They turn out to parallel developing events that continue across considerable time in the life span. These periodic conjunctions make it impossible that someone other than Shakespeare wrote the plays, or that he might be referring to completely other events than what is evidenced by the little that is available in the life-text. However, we have to be cautious what we say about how Shakespeare felt, or what he was trying to do. But even here common sense allows us to reach certain conclusions.

Shakespeare found having twins a striking phenomenon with legal and psychological as well as biological and economic implications. That he was negatively affected by the loss of his only son is so without a shadow of a doubt, but we can also discern some positive compensation. He is sexually nervous about his daughters' chastity, as he is guilty about his lack of it (*Measure, Cleopatra, Sonnets*). None of these art works is a photograph but more of a Rausche dot. But this analysis, hopefully, will provide more historical, political, legal, biographical and familial contexts for his plays, which are so often treated in such unnecessary isolation. Above all, that thing most everyone is uncomfortable about is acknowledging that the author existed. It is inexcusable to contribute to the false idea that we know little about him or he attempted to abide our question, or had no ideas of his own. These new insights may bring us closer to discovering why great minds during his lifetime were, and since are, willing to give so much of their time to him; not merely to be entertained, but to learn some things extremely well through a number of plays. It is a good antidote to the idea that he wrote his plays for pedestrians in the audiences at the Globe to remember that his *first* play was performed at Gray's Inn and his last in Whitehall, both of these before the then reigning monarchs. More relevant to our subthemes is to remind ourselves that he would presume that every performance of any play would find in the audiences graduates of the London law schools, and whenever he put pen to paper he had reason to be concerned about his mother's inheritance to him, or his to his offspring. His very use of intertextuality from law-texts in his play-texts helped produce the income to replace his father's losses in order to pass on their substitution in his own estate to his heirs.

The plays reveal a development or maturing from the early plays where he encounters his losses and legal entanglements. In the middle plays he discerns that the play-text substitutes for life-text losses. The later plays evidence his self-conscious capacity to see that fiction only proves it is a substitution and allows one to explore one's intentions only to discover one's own counter-intentionalities. Only when he begins to stop writing and looks back on his last plays does he realize that they have been mapping and mirroring his own life-concerns. He also had the compensation from his work to know, that now written and performed, it continued to have its own life before King James, as it revealed that his concerns became those of the Monarch and legal history. We finally can admit that even if some of Shakespeare's autobiographical moments creep into the plays, they are also part of the small tradition of twins at the Inns in drama, the middle ground tradition of mercy- and justice-figures in Medieval and Renaissance periods. From an even greater perspective, Shakespeare appears to be part of the cycles of dramatic and literary responses to the rise and fall of equity concepts in the history of the interplay between law and drama.

Often we allow the discernment of these literary and historic traditions through source, genre, and topical studies to obliterate the autobiographical facts instrumental in producing the works of these modes in the first place. We can only begin to appreciate Shakespeare as a source for observing human patterns, or recurring personal problems with their resolutions, if we can perceive how he was learning to do this for himself in his own fiction.

Notes

Introduction

1. "Introduction," *Selections from the Essays of Montaigne*, N.Y. 1948. Cf. Also Michael Neill, "The World Beyond: Shakespeare and the Tropes of Translation," *Elizabethan Theater: Essays in Honor of S. Schoenbaum*, eds. R. B. Parker and S. P. Pitner, University of Delaware Press, 1996.

2. W. Nicholas Knight, "Shakespeare's Signature in Two Florio's Montaigne's *Essays, Manuscripta*, St. Louis University, Missouri, 1997, presented at Manuscripta Conference October, 1996; earlier report "New Shakespeare 'Signature': Image or Autograph," *Images of Shakespeare* Seminar in Berlin at Third Congress of the International Shakespeare Association, 1986 *Images of Shakespeare*, ed. Habicht, Palmer and Pringle, University of Delaware Press, 1988, p.344.

3. And Richard P. Wheeler, *The Whole Journey: Shakespeare's Power of Development*, University of California Press, 1986, pp. 53-54.

4. *A Study of Dramatic Form and its Relation to Social Custom*, Princeton University Press, 1959.

5. *Studies in Literature: A Journal of Interdisciplinary Criticism*, ed. Leonard F. Manheim, University of Hartford, Vol. IX, Nos. 2-3, 1977.

6. Richard A. Posner, *Law and Literature: A Misunderstood Relation*, Harvard University Press, 1988; Daniel J. Kornstein, *Kill All the Lawyers: Shakespeare's Legal Appeal*, Princeton University Press, 1994; Eric Sams, *The Real Shakespeare—Retrieving the Early Years, 1564-1594*, Yale University Press, 1995; *Law and Literature Perspectives*, ed. Bruce L. Rockwood, Peter Lang, N.Y., 1996; and W. Nicholas Knight, *Shakespeare's Hidden Life: Shakespeare at the Law 1585-1595*, Mason & Lipscomb, N.Y., 1973.

7. "The Good, the Bad, and the Ironic: Two Views on Law and Literature", *Yale Journal of Law and the Humanities*, Summer, 1996, Vol. 8:2, p. 558.

Chapter I: Shakespeare's Court Case

1. Portions of this chapter appeared in *Law and Critique*, Vol. II, No. 1, Spring, Department of Law, University of Lancaster, U.K., Deborah Charles Publications, Liverpool, 1991. Originally presented in a Law Seminar of Shakespeare Association of America Meetings of 1989 in Austin, Texas.

2. "The Birth of the Author", Parker, *Elizabethan Theatre*, p. 90.

3. "Constructing the Author", *Ibid.*, pp. 93-100.

4. Ian Donaldson, "Jonson and the Tother Youth", pp. 111-129.

5. "The Presence of the Playwright, 1580-1640", pp. 130-146.

6. *The Aims of Interpretation*, University of Chicago Press, p. 2.

7. Since "counter-intentionality" is a concept of interest in Chapters III-VI a brief explanation of its presence in Shakespeare's plays may be helpful at this point. "Intentionality" is a character making apparent what their plans, purposes, or goals are. "Counter-intentionality" is the reversing of the hidden, suppressed, and for the most part, opposing purposes within the character to that declared intent. A brief example from *Julius Caesar* will suffice to illustrate "counter-intentionality" being dramatized by Shakespeare (quotations from Shakespeare come from *The Complete Works of Shakespeare* ed. David Bevington, 4th edition, Scott, Foresman and Company, Longman, N.Y., 1997.)

> Brutus. Our [the conspirators'] course will seem too bloody, Caius Cassius,
> To cut the head [Caesar] off and then hack the limbs [Antony],
> Like wrath in death and envy afterwords;...
> And let our hearts, as subtle masters do,
> Stir up their servants to an act of rage,
> And after seem to chide 'em. This shall make
> Our purpose necessary and not envious...
>   II.i. 162-164, 175-178
> Antony. This was the noblest Roman of them all:
> All the conspirators save only he

Did that they did in envy of great Caesar

V.iv. 68-70

Shakespeare has shown Brutus concluding "It must be by his death: and for my part,/I know no personal cause to spurn at him,..." and continuing to fail to find any impersonal reason ("...since the Quarrel/Will bear no colour for the thing he is,/Fashion it thus;..." (II.i. 10-34). Thus Shakespeare has dramatized Antony's seeing through Brutus' fashioning of the conspiracy's intents to appear as if they were for the *general* good. Antony disclosed the "counter-intentionality" behind the assassination as *personal* envy, earlier captured in Cassius' "and this man/Is now become a god" speech (I.ii. 90-161). Shakespeare's text, as opposed to Plutarch's as his source, has thus revealed a Brutus whose intents are fashioned as honorable but have personal counter-intentionality.

Likewise Hamlet intends to kill Claudius but an Oedipal reading suggests his counter-intentionality envies Claudius' killing of his father and marrying his mother, thereby paralyzing his action. Macbeth envies Duncan's power but his ambitious desires may be driving him as they ironically do, to obtain nothing ("I have no spur/To prick the sides of my intent, but only/Vaulting ambition, which o'er leaps itself/And falls on th' other." (I.vii. 25-28)

Othello loves "too well" Desdemona and murders her. And we shall see Lear wants love from two of his daughters and gets unimagined hate.

Shakespeare's tragedies are the consequences of the revelation in the heroes of their counter-intentionality. Shakespeare's comedies are the characters' overcoming through the domination of their intent to discover lost children, consummate love in marriage, reveal mistaken identities and show how mercy and equity can prevail in human affairs. This comic triumph occurs after the intervention of counter-intentionality caused by the loss of children, siblings, justice and, through manipulations caused by law, hate and misunderstandings.

8. Robert Scholes, *Textual Power: Literary Theory and the Teaching of English*, Yale University Press, New Haven, 1985, p. 40.

9. Virginia Woolf, *A Room of One's Own*, pp. 43-44.

10. Martin Heidegger, "The Origin of the Work of Art", *Poetry, Language, Thought*, trans. Albert Hofstadter, N.Y., 1971, pp. 15-85.

11. *Shakespeare Newsletter*, April, 1974, p. 11.

12. cf. Posner, pp. 90-99 and John Gross, *Shylock: Four Hundred Years in the Life of a Legend*, Vintage, London, 1994, pp. 63-68.

13. cf. Mark Edwin Andrews, *Law versus Equity in The Merchant of Venice*, Boulder, 1965 and Godfrey Davies, *The Early Stuarts* 1603-1660, Oxford, 1959, p. 88.

14. Elaborated at greater length in my *Shakespeare's Hidden Life*, pp. 103-156, 218-227.

15. *Progresses of Queen Elizabeth*, ed. I.Nichols, A-H, London, 1788, p. 41.

16. W. J. Jones, *The Elizabethan Court of Chancery*, Oxford, Clarendon Press, 1967, pp. 436-437.

17. G. W. Keeton, "Shakespeare at Law", *Anglo American Law Review*, April 1974, No. 36.

Chapter II: Twins at the Inns of Court

1. Portions of this chapter appeared as "Comic Twins at the Inns of Court", in *Publications of Missouri Philological Association*, 4-1947, pp. 74-82.

2. Particularly Sam Schoenbaum, *William Shakespeare: A Compact Documentary Life*, Oxford, 1977, pp. 30-44, 94.

3. Henry Holmes, who served as the Prince of Purpoole for that year. *Gesta Grayorium*, London, not published until 1688.

4. Philip J. Finkelpearl, *John Marston of the Middle Temple*, Cambridge, Mass., 1969, pp. 42-43. *The Duchess of Malfi* has twins as major characters and Webster is believed to have been the John Webster matriculated at the Temple. Dramatists such as Ben Jonson, Thomas Middleton and others were also associated with the Inns of Court. cf. Middleton's *Michaelmas Term* and W. Nicholas Knight, "Sex and Law Language in Middleton's *Michaelmas Term*",

"Accompaninge the Players": *Essays Celebrating Thomas Middleton, 1580-1980*, ed. Kenneth Friedenreich, AMS Press, N. Y., 1983, pp. 89-108.

5. *The Complete Works of Shakespeare*, ed. Hardin Craig, Scott Foresman, Chicago, 1951, p. 615.

6. *Ibid*, p. 615.

7. cf. Edward J. White, *Commentaries on the Law in Shakespeare*. St. Louis, 1911, pp. 34-41; cites how numerous, widespread and far-ranging the legal references are in all of Shakespeare's works.

8. Northrop Frye, *Anatomy of Criticism*, Princeton, (1957) 1971.

9. "An Essay on the Sonnets", *The Sonnets of Shakespeare*, Dell, N. Y., 1960, pp. 7-33.

10. "John Updike", *Writers at Work: The Paris Review Interviews*, Fourth Series, ed. George Plimpton, p. 444.

11. cf. W. Nicholas Knight, "The Narrative Unity of Book V of *The Faerie Queene*: 'That Part of Justice Which is Equity'", *The Review of English Studies*, New Series, Vol. XXI, No. 83, August, 1970, pp. 267-294 and A. C. Hamilton, "Introduction: Book V", *Spenser: The Faerie Queene*, Longman, London, 1980, pp. 525-526.

12. Arthur F. Kinney talks about Shakespeare "ranging resources of kind" (p. 31) and "the mixing of kinds" (p. 33) with regard to these tensions in *Comedy of Errors*; cf. "Shakespeare's *Comedy of Errors* and the Nature of Kinds", *Studies in Philology*, LXXXV, No. 1 (Winter, 1988) pp. 29-52 and recently a subject of discussion at a conference organized by the University of Massachusetts Center for Renaissance Studies on "Cultural Exchanges" November 14-17, 1996 at Amherst, MA. and at Mount Holyoke and Smith Colleges.

Chapter III: A Son's Loss and Compensation

1. Portions of the chapter on *Twelfth Night* originate in a paper entitled "Weave Their Thread with Bones" presented in "Shakespeare and Psychology" at the American Shakespeare Association Meetings in Cambridge, Massachusetts, April 19-21,

1984 and appeared as "Shakespeare's Mourning for his Son in *Twelfth Night*" in *Comments on Literature*, #3, ed. Gerald Cohen, Rolla, Missouri, November 1, 1984. pp 1-9. Earlier analysis of *Merchant of Venice* by me appeared as "Merchant of Venice as a Reflection of Shakespeare's Personal Losses", *Comments on Literature* #4, November 15, 1985, pp. 19-25 (#3 and #4 are supplements to *Comments on Etymology* edited by Professor Cohen). See also W. Nicholas Knight, "Equity, The *Merchant of Venice* and William Lambarde", *Shakespeare Survey 27*, ed. Kenneth Muir, Cambridge University Press, 1974, pp. 93-104. Note: Lawrence Danson, *The Harmonies of the Merchant of Venice*, Yale University Press, 1978, p. 83.

2. A. L. Rowse, *William Shakespeare*, N. Y., 1964, p. 35.

3. E. A. J. Honigmann, "The Second-Best Bed", *New York Review of Books*, November 7, 1991, pp. 27-30 and see also Stanley Wells, *Shakespeare's Lives: 1991-1994, Elizabethan Theatre*, ed. Parker, pp. 18-22, and Honigmann's *Shakespeare: The Lost Years* and "There Is a World Elsewhere: William Shakespeare, Businessman," *Images of Shakespeare: Proceedings of the Third Congress of the International Shakespeare Association*, 1986 in Berlin, eds. Werner Habicht, D. J. Palmer, and Roger Pringle, University of Delaware Press, Newark, 1988, pp. 40-46.

4. cf. Leslie Hotson's *Shakespeare versus Shallow*, Boston: Litttle Brown, 1931.

5. C. L. Barber's "Ch. 10: Testing Courtesy and Humanity in *Twelfth Night*", *Shakespeare's Festive Comedy* and Joseph H. Summers, "The Masks of *Twelfth Night*", *Shakespeare: Modern Essays in Criticism*, ed. Leonard F. Dean, Oxford, 1967, pp. 134-143.

6. cf. *King John* (1596) III.iv. 47-104.

7. *Anatomy of Criticism*, pp. 163-164.

8. *Shakespeare's Festive Comedy*, p. 238.

9. The significance of this initial placement of these references cannot be overemphasized. The shaping importance of Shakespeare's beginnings is well documented in Willson's Introduction and the

essays in *Entering the Maze: Shakespeare's Art of Beginning*, ed. Robert F. Willson, Jr., Peter Lang Publishing, N. Y., 1995.

10. As found in Andrews, *Law versus Equity...*, p. 40. cf. also Stephen A. Cohen, "'The Quality of Mercy': Law, Equity and Ideology in *The Merchant of Venice"*, *Adversaria: Literature and Law*, ed. Evelyn J. Hinz, University of Manitoba, Winnipeg 27/4 December 1994, pp. 35-54.

11. As Shakespeare explores in his drama with the instrument of one of his characters he probes their intent and their "counter-intention-ality". Counter-intentionality is discovered as a character reveals what he or she is intending to do or say about a concept in their search for law, justice, equity, mercy or proper inheritance, the significance of gifts and giving in a Will out of caring or love. Shakespeare has the character encounter in such revelation the exposure and betrayal of their intents' opposites. This may be evidenced in their inadvertently pursuing nothingness, purely personal motives, chaos, disorder, dissolution, evil, injustice, iniquity, inequity, hate, envy and ingratitude. These well up in human consciousness as the opposite of what the character intended to motivate or instigate. Civilization and personality tend to suppress these opposites from appearing in consciousness or action. They appear in humanity as a correlative to physics as if obeying the laws of Newton--for every action there is an equal and opposite reaction. Intent is what we want and counter-intent is what we have to repress to get it. Shakespearean tragedies show counter-intentionality winning and his comedies the victory of good intent.

Chapter IV:
Before King James: Betrayal and Revelation

1. Some of this material on *Measure for Measure* was initially presented in a paper for Maurice Charney's Comedy Seminar in San Francisco meetings of the Shakespeare Association of America, 1979 and published as "Shakespeare Before King James: Betrayal and Revelation" in *Iowa State Journal of Research*, February 1988, Vol. 62, No. 3, pp. 387-395.

2. George Garrett, *Death of the Fox*, New York, 1971, p. 25.

3. cf. Samuel E. Thorne, Preface to Hake's *Epiekeia*, [Greek for "equity"], Yale, 1953, p. v. Cf. Knight, *Shakespeare's Hidden Life*, pp. 137, 176, 185, 190, 229-233. For a discussion of equity of statute exercised by the interpretation of Praetori in Rome and Chancellors in England cf. H. Maine, "Ancient Law", in *The Legal Imagination*, James B. White, pp. 651-655.

4. Josephine Waters Bennett, *"Measure for Measure" as Royal Entertainment*, Columbia University Press, 1966. Most recent recognition of the legal complexity and ambiguity in *Measure for Measure* is found in Ervene Gulley, "Dressed in a Little Brief Authority"; Law as Theater in *Measure for Measure* in *Law and Literature Perspectives*, ed., Bruce L. Rockwood, Peter Lang, N.Y., 1996, pp. 53-80.

5. The passage and excellent discussion are found in Andrews, *Law versus Equity*...p. 40. An earlier study of equity in Shakespeare is Charles E. Phelps, *Falstaff and Equity*, Boston, 1902.

6. Alvin Kernan, *Shakespeare, The King's Playwright*, Yale University Press, 1995.

7. For more specific examples see David M. Bergeron, *Shakespeare's Romances and the Royal Family*, University of Kansas Press, 1985; note Ellesmere's "Speech before Parliament on *Post Nati*" and Shakespeare's use of it as historic backgrounding for *Cymbeline* with the character of Posthumus.

Chapter V: His Daughters and Last Plays

1. Some of this chapter's material appeared in "Patrimony and Shakespeare's Daughters" I presented at MLA, December 27, 1977 at the second meeting on Law and Literature, with Richard Weisberg and James Boyd White published in University of Hartford *Studies in Literature*, pp. 175-186. For essays from a psychoanalytical approach to Shakespeare's use of family in his plays see *Representing Shakespeare: New Psychoanalytic Essays*, eds. Murray M. Schwarz and Coppelia Kahn, Johns Hopkins University Press, Baltimore, 1980. The classic on these subjects is

Norman Holland's *Psychoanalysis and Shakespeare*, New York: Octagon Books, 1976.

2. See Edward J. White, *Commentaries on the Law in Shakespeare*, St. Louis, 1911.

3. "The Nature of Topicality in *Love's Labour's Lost*", *Shakespeare Survey 38*, Cambridge University Press, 1985, p. 59.

4. Schoenbaum, *Shakespeare's Lives*, p. 27.

5. Burgess, *Shakespeare*, N. Y., 1970, p. 254.

6. Cf. above, Burgess and Schoenbaum.

Chapter VI: Life-Text in Play-Text

1. Among others, Sams and Honigmann think so. The most sensible and reasonable biography assuming Shakespeare to be the author of his plays is Anthony Holden's *William Shakespeare: The Man Behind the Genius*, Little Brown, N.Y., 2000, influenced by the fine work of Frank Kermode.

2. Christopher Hill, *The Century of Revolution: 1603-1714*, Thomas Nelson and Sons Ltd.,Edinburgh, 1961, p. 96.

3. Ben Jonson, *Bartholomew Fair*, eds., C. H. Herford and P. and E. Simpson, *Five Plays*, Oxford, 1959, p. 477, II.i.7-9.

Works Cited

Andrews, Mark Edwin, *Law versus Equity in The Merchant of Venice*, Boulder, Colorado, 1965.

Barber, C. L., "An Essay on the Sonnets", *The Sonnets of Shakespeare*, ed. Charles Jasper Sisson, Dell, N. Y., 1960, pp. 7-33.

———. *Shakespeare's Festive Comedy*, Princeton University Press, 1959.

———. and Richard P. Wheeler, *The Whole Journey*, University of California Press, Berkeley, 1986.

Bennett, Josephine Waters, *"Measure for Measure" as Royal Entertainment*, Columbia University Press, 1966.

Bergeron, David M., *Shakespeare's Romances and the Royal Family*, University of Kansas Press, Lawerence, 1985.

Burgess, Anthony, *Shakespeare*, Alfred Knopf, N. Y., 1970.

Cohen, Stephen A., "'The Quality of Mercy': Law, Equity and Ideology in *The Merchant of Venice*" *Adversaria: Literature and Law*, ed. Evelyn J. Hinz, *Mosaic* 27/4 Dec., 1994, pp. 35-54.

The Complete Shakespeare, ed. David Bevington, 4th edition, Longman, N. Y., 1997.

The Complete Works of Shakespeare, ed. Hardin Craig, Scott Foresman, Chicago, 1951.

Danson, Lawrence, *The Harmonies of the Merchant of Venice*, Yale University Press, 1978.

Davies, Godfrey, *The Early Stuarts 1603-1660*, Oxford, 1959.

Entering the Maze: Shakespeare's Art of Beginning, ed. Robert F. Willson, Jr., Peter Lang Publishing, N. Y., 1995.

Finkelpearl, Philip J., *John Marston of the Middle Temple*, Cambridge, Mass., 1969.

Frame, Donald M., *Selections From the Essays of Montaigne*, Appleton-Century-Crofts, New York, 1948.

Frye, Northrop, *Anatomy of Criticism*, Princeton University Press, 1971.

Garrett, George, *Death of the Fox*, New York, 1971, P. 25.

Gross, John, *Shylock: Four Hundred Years in the Life of a Legend*, Vintage, London, 1994.

Hamilton, A. C., "Introduction: Book V", *Spenser: The Faerie Queene*, Longman, London, 1980, pp. 525-526.

Heidegger, Martin, "The Origin of the Work of Art", *Poetry, Language, Thought*, trans. Albert Hofstadter, N. Y., 1971, pp. 15-85.

Helmes, Henry, *Gesta Grayorium*, London, 1688.

Hill, Christopher, *The Century of Revolution: 1603-1714*, Edinburgh, 1961.

Hirsch, Eric Donald, *The Aims of Interpretation*, University of Chicago Press, 1976.

116

Holden, Anthony, *William Shakespeare: The Man Behind the Genius*, Little Brown, N.Y., 2000.

Holland, Norman, *Psychoanalysis and Shakespeare*, New York: Octagon Books, 1976.

Honigmann, E. A. J. "The Second Best Bed", *New York Review of Books*, November 7, 1991, pp. 27-30.

Hotson, Leslie, *Shakespeare versus Shallow*, Little Brown, Boston, 1931.

Images of Shakespeare: Proceedings of the Third Congress of the International Shakespeare Association, 1986, eds. Werner Habicht, D. J. Palmer and Roger Pringle, University of Delaware, 1988.

Jones, W. J., *The Elizabethan Court of Chancery*, Oxford, Clarendon Press, 1967.

Jonson, Ben, *Bartholomew Fair*, eds., C. H. Herford and P. and E. Simpson *Five Plays*, Oxford, 1959, p. 477, II.i.7-9.

Keeton, G. W., "Shakespeare at Law", *Anglo American Law Review*, April 1974, No. 36.

Kernan, Alvin, *Shakespeare, The King's Playwright*, Yale University Press, 1995.

Kinney, Arthur F., "Shakespeare's *Comedy of Errors* and the Nature of Kinds", *Studies in Philology*, LXXXV, No. 1 (Winter, 1988), pp. 29-52.

Knight, W. Nicholas, "Comic Twins at the Inns of Court", *Publications of Missouri Philological Association* 4: pp. 74-82.

———. "Equity, *The Merchant of Venice* and William Lambarde", *Shakespeare Survey* 27, ed. Kenneth Muir, Cambridge University Press, 1974, pp. 93-104.

———. "*Merchant of Venice* as a Reflection of Shakespeare's Personal Losses", *Comments on Literature* #4 (Supplement to *Comments on Etymology*), ed. Gerald Cohen, Rolla, MO, Nov. 15, 1985, pp. 19-25.

———. "The Narrative Unity of Book V of *The Faerie Queene*: 'That Part of Justice Which is Equity'", *The Review of English Studies*, Oxford New Series, Vol. XXI, No. 83, August, 1970, pp. 267-294.

———. "Sex and Law Language in Middleton's *Michaelmas Term*", *"Accomaninge the Players"*: *Essays Celebrating Thomas Middleton, 1580-1980*, ed. Kenneth Friedenreick, AMS Press, N. Y., 1983, pp. 89-108.

———. "Shakespeare Before King James: Betrayal and Revelation", *Iowa State Journal of Research*, February 1988, Vol. 62, No. 3, pp. 387-395.

———. "Shakespeare's Court Case", *Law and Critique*, Vol. II, No. 1, Liverpool, Spring 1991, pp. 103-112.

———. *Shakespeare's Hidden Life: Shakespeare at the Law 1585-1595*, Mason C. Lipscomb, N.Y., 1973.

———. "Shakespeare's Mourning for His Son in *Twelfth Night*", *Comments on Literature* #3 (Supplement to *Comments on Etymology*), ed. Gerald Cohen, Rolla, Missouri, Nov. 1, 1984, pp. 1-9.

Kornstein, Daniel J., *Kill All The Lawyers: Shakespeare's Legal Appeal*, Princeton University Press, 1994.

Lamb, Mary Ellen, "The Nature of Topicality in *Love's Labour's Lost*", *Shakespeare Survey* 38, Cambridge University Press, 1985, pp. 49-59.

Law and Literature Perspectives, ed. Bruce L. Rockwood, Peter Lang, N.Y., 1996.

Parker, R. B and S. P. Zitner eds., *Elizabethan Theater*, University of Delaware Press, Newark, 1996.

Phelps, Charles E., *Falstaff and Equity*, Boston, 1902.

Posner, Richard A., *Law and Literature: A Misunderstood Relation*, Harvard University Press, 1988.

Progresses of Queen Elizabeth, ed. I. Nichols, A-H, London, 1796.

Representing Shakespeare: New Psychoanalytic Essays, eds. Murray M. Schwarz and Coppelia Kahn, Johns Hopkins University Press, Baltimore, 1980.

Rockwood, Bruce L., "The Good, the Bad, and the Ironic: Two Views on Law and Literature", *Yale Journal of Law and the Humanities*, Summer, 1996, pp. 533-558.

Sams, Eric, *The Real Shakespeare: Retrieving the Early Years, 1564-1594*, Yale University Press, 1995.

Schoenbaum, Sam, *Shakespeare: A Documentary Life*, Oxford, 1975.

———. *Shakespeare: Records and Images*, Oxford, 1981.

———. *Shakespeare: Lives*, updated 1991, Oxford.

———. *William Shakespeare: A Compact Documentary Life*, Oxford, 1977.

Scholes, Robert, *Textual Power: Literary Theory and the Teaching of English*, Yale University Press, New Haven, 1985.

Shakespeare Newsletter, Ed. Louis Marder, University of Illinois, April 1974.

Studies in Literature, ed. Leonard F. Manheim, University of Hartford, Vol. IX, Nos. 2-3, 1977.

Summers, Joseph H., "The Masks of *Twelfth Night*", *Shakespeare Modern Essays in Criticism*, ed. Leonard F. Dean, Oxford, 1967, pp. 134-143.

Thorne, Samuel E., Preface, *Hake's Epiekeia*, Yale, 1953.

Updike, John, "John Updike", *Writers at Work: The Paris Review Interviews*, Fourth Series, ed. George Plimpton, pp. 431-454.

West, William, *Symboleography*, London, 1594.

White, Edward J., *Commentaries on the Law in Shakespeare*, St. Louis, 1911.

White, James Boyd, *The Legal Imagination*, Boston, 1973.

Woolf, Virginia, *A Room of One's Own*, N.Y., 1957.

Index